HOW TO CHEAT AT GARDENING

You don't want to spend your time bending over plants that will, mysteriously, die on you given the slightest chance; or cutting a lawn that seems to grow faster than anyone else's; or tying up the roses round the door because they're threatening to come *in*doors and join the rest of the family in the living-room. You don't see yourself waltzing round the lawn, trug basket in hand, cutting flowers, either.

But you do get a conscience about it all. You hate to admit it, but you do. Your garden is the one that stands out from the rest when you see it from the train – like an unmade bed in a hospital ward. Your front garden is in imminent danger of becoming *the* courting ground for all the local cats (no one can spot them in all that long grass) and, worse still, people are beginning to mistake the back for a patch of waste ground, and are throwing beer bottles and fish and chip papers over your hedge.

So what are you going to do about it?
You are going to cheat. You will make your particular patch of ground look good, and cared for, you will keep it under, but you will do so with the absolute minimum of effort. You're going to garden the lazy way.

Also available in Coronet Books:

How to Cheat at Cooking

How to Cheat at Gardening

Hazel Evans

CORONET BOOKS
Hodder and Stoughton

First published in Great Britain in 1971
by Ebury Press

Coronet edition 1976
Second impression 1976

Line drawings by Wendy Jones

Printed and bound in Great Britain for
Coronet Books, Hodder and Stoughton, London.
By Hunt Barnard Printing Ltd.,
Aylesbury, Bucks.

ISBN 0 340 20578 4

To Harry, who does
(cheat at gardening)

CONTENTS

INTRODUCTION

My first thoughts on gardening were sheer terror, when I was taken as a toddler round the country estate my grandfather managed. There was the frightening jungle where the orchids grew, and steam came hissing out of hot pipes. There was the sickening scent of the geraniums in the greenhouse, standing to attention, waiting to be bedded out. And, outside, there were the red-hot pokers and tiger lilies towering over me, menacing and unreal.

Shame and embarrassment – as only a nine-year-old can experience them – followed later on when one of my more eccentric aunts, a Fellow of the Royal Horticultural Society, took me to Wisley. I was made to keep watch while she skittered about in the bushes, stealing seed pods from unobtainable exotic shrubs, and handed them to me with hissed instructions to put them in my mac pocket. She could grow anything. All I could grow was budgerigar seed plants which had blood-red sap.

Hate set in when my father acquired an allotment some distance from home. Every time I wanted to go out and play, I was despatched on my bike to cut a cabbage for lunch. The soil was sticky clay and clung to my shoes, the cabbages were leathery and obstinate, and the weather was invariably rainy and cold. I vowed then that when I grew up I would live in a flat and never grow a thing.

But I came from a long line of impassioned gardeners, and during my Wild Oat period, when I worked in the country, I took on a mini-smallholding. I grew shallots for the local sausage factory and raised pigs, too – until the lorry came to take them away for slaughter and I collapsed in tears. After I married, I again got farming mania, which culminated in the terrible Summer of the Broad Bean, when there was such a glut that I couldn't even give our crop away, and had to plough it into the ground.

And now? Gardening has become a simply splendid, relaxing pastime in spring and summer when the mood takes over and a little fresh air is indicated. But when it's cold and damp, when there's a gale blowing, and there's an intriguing old film to watch on the telly, Sunday afternoons spent close to the soil have less appeal.

That's what this book is about. I've tried to take the slog out of gardening, with tips gleaned from my own experiences, so that you don't plant things that are petulant and need regular devoted care, but choose instead plants you can attend to when *you* feel like doing so. You never know, you might even get to *enjoy* gardening in time!

1
WHAT IT'S ALL ABOUT

There are two kinds of gardeners: the "Dig-a-double-trench" and "Aren't-my-dahlias-lovely" brigade – and the rest of us. For let's face it, doing the garden is either your life-long relaxation and hobby (in which case you won't be reading *this* book), or just another household chore like washing the car, which you are shamed into tackling when the view from your back window begins to look like something from a bad science fiction film.

It's not until the columbine and the couch grass start actually growing *over* your back doorstep that you feel something has to be done about it? Right, then this book is for you.

So now you've admitted it, and you feel better: you hate gardening. You prefer to spend your week-ends sailing or playing golf, or visiting friends, or simply blissfully doing nothing at all.

You don't want to spend your time bending over plants that will, mysteriously, die on you given the slightest chance; or cutting a lawn that seems to grow faster than anyone else's; or tying up the roses round the door because they're threatening to come *in*doors and join the rest of the family in the living-room. You don't see yourself waltzing round the lawn, trug basket in hand, cutting flowers, either.

But you do get a conscience about it all. You hate to admit it, but you do. Your garden is the one that stands out from the rest when you see it from the train – like an unmade bed in a hospital ward. Your front garden is in imminent danger of becoming *the* courting ground for all the local cats (no one can spot them in all that long grass;) and, worse still, people are beginning to mistake the back for a patch of waste ground, and are throwing beer bottles and fish and chip papers over your hedge.

I once went to a cocktail party in Hampstead which was held in a garden that was immaculately kept. The one next door was not. It was a wilderness, a positive cats' paradise. One by one, the cigarette-smokers among us, afraid to damage our host's pristine lawn, started furtively using the next-door garden as a giant ash tray, slinging cigarette butts and empty packets over the fence. Soon everyone was doing it. I doubt if the owner was amused the next morning, when he surveyed the scene from his back window. But that's the kind of thing that happens if your garden gets out of hand.

"My, you've got a job on *there*, haven't you!" is one of the favourite phrases used by Jonah-like friends who come to view your new house and garden.

"Yes; like to come and help?" is all that you can say, tersely, in reply.

"That ground elder's getting a hold, isn't it?" remarks your next-door neighbour nervously, peering over the fence. He's got a vested interest in that ground elder, of course. He's afraid it will come up into *his* garden sooner or later, and he's probably right. He's trying to shame you into digging it up. But you know that, by your present methods, as fast as you tug at those terrible underground stems, twice as many will crop up in their place.

So what are you going to do about it?

You are going to cheat. You will make your particular patch of ground look good, and cared for, you will keep it under, but you will do so with the absolute minimum of effort. You're going to garden the lazy way.

The neighbours' immaculate gardens show up your own . . .

What you're not aiming at

The average suburban garden is nothing much more than a status symbol, like a shiny new car that the owner can't quite afford. Or it can be an outlet for frustration – the man who can't be master in his own house will take it out on the garden instead. He'll keep it ferociously tidy, pinning down plants, chopping off branches, hacking down undergrowth. And he'll grow the biggest vegetable marrows for miles around – taking all the prizes at the local show, when he should be shot for letting anything grow so large and so tasteless.

My grandfather once grew a marrow that was so big they had to move it on a wheelbarrow. But when my grandmother came to cook it, or part of it, its flesh was so tough and stringy and inedible that they had to feed it to the pigs. Don't copy that example. If you must grow marrows (and I can't for the life of me think why anyone wants to), chop them off when they get to courgette size and poach them in butter. If you want to grow something for status purposes, grow gourds instead – at least you don't have to eat them afterwards.

At one time I lived in a shipyard town in the North of England. The men there were all henpecked out of their lives by fearsome wives (I know – one of them was my landlady), who wore their hair in curlers all day long and stood, arms crossed, on the doorstep waiting for their men to come home.

What did the husbands do when they couldn't escape to the pub or to the dogs? They grew dahlias and chrysanthemums in the backyard, huge, hideous, earwiggy things. And each man had to have a bigger and better display than his neighbour.

Those flowers weren't grown to be cut and used in the house, they weren't even grown to make the yard look pretty. They were grown simply for their size. You'd see the men out there measuring them up, choosing them for the flower show. And on the night before the big event, some of the husbands used to sit out instead of sleeping, guarding their plants in case a jealous rival damaged them. For some people had actually been known to pour weed-killer over the fence.

You're never going to be like that. What you want is a garden that doesn't worry you. But if you want to get one up on your gardening friends, I'm going to show you some ways to do that, too. Have you ever seen a Michaelmas daisy tree, for instance? Or a climbing chrysanthemum? You can find out how to grow them later on. So don't sublimate your feelings of aggression on your poor plants – it would be healthier to go out and work them off on the golf course or the tennis court instead.

You're going to plan your garden for leisure and pleasure. But that doesn't mean you need rush out there, spade in hand, and attack the thing in a frenzy of guilt. Instead, you will use cunning. You'll take a long, hard look at the kind of garden you've already got, then remodel it the lazy gardener's way.

You're going to borrow from your neighbours, too. If the family next door are fools enough to spend hours slaving over their garden, bedding out plants and pruning trees, horn in on them. Enjoy the view, too, instead of shutting it off with a high fence.

A lot of people waste no end of time and money putting a great high wall up around their plot. It's not only expensive, but it's sheer hell to maintain, especially if it is made of wood. It will make your garden look smaller than it actually is, too, and will keep out half the sun. Then you'll need to spend a fortune growing things against it to hide its ugliness. If it's privacy you're after, all you need to avoid those unwanted over-the-fence gossip sessions is one high piece of screening just at the back of the house.

After all, you can build walls a dozen feet high round your garden, but if the people next door are all *that* keen to look, they have only to go to their bedroom window to see what you're up to, anyway!

The picture-in-a-frame garden

So how are you going to cope with this jungle you've inherited, or this balding patch of rock-strewn rubble? First of all you've got to ask yourself one important question: What do I want the garden *for*?

So you just want a view? You may rarely want to go out into your garden at all. You may simply want to look at it. In your life, if you're both working, if you're away at week-ends, or busy boating, your garden may simply be a view from the back windows.

Come to think of it, you may not even *like* going out into your garden: the noise of jets screaming overhead may make life impossible out there, or for all I know you may live next to a glue factory. What you need, then, is nothing more than a pretty view to be framed by your kitchen window, something that's pleasant to look at without shouting reminders at you that it needs attention.

You'll want something that will give you colour all the year round, and plants that are neat and not too tiresome to deal with. If your garden is simply going to be like a picture on the wall, you may not even need grass. It could be simply a nuisance from your point of view, when there are other carpeting plants that will do the job better and need no cutting.

For the picture garden the plants and shrubs you choose must be able to take care of themselves as much as possible, and since they are going to be seen from a long distance, they need to be largish in scale. There's no point in planting coy little clumps of snowdrops, for instance, if they are going to flower unseen. But you can have fun with colour – try clumps of flowers all in one shade. You can choose plants with exciting shapes too.

Scope for outdoor living

Or do you want an outdoor room? This could be just what you're looking for if you plan to loll about in your garden, eat meals in it, take naps in it, entertain friends in it. If that's the case, then you must re-think your ideas on gardening altogether and plan instead in terms of an extra room for the house – for that's what it becomes.

Your garden will need interior decorating, and you can experiment with colour, while you're about it. You can give it a theme – a Mediterranean look, for instance, if you can afford plenty of patio material. You'll certainly need something more than an ordinary suburban

See that garden or patio furniture is weatherproof

garden look to fill the bill – and the bill will, in your case, include some garden furniture. For (up to a point) the more non-growing, inanimate things you can get into your plot, the better. Ponds, fountains, statues – the lot – all help to make it look good and need little or no looking after. But don't feel that you are stuck with concrete windmills and plastic gnomes – they're surprisingly pricy, anyway. A phone call to the local School of Art could find you an enthusiastic young sculptor with nowhere to display his wares, who might make something for you just as cheaply.

What you *don't* want to buy, let me say here and now, is any form of garden furniture that will rust, that will need repainting (sheer murder, all the paint drips on to the grass) or lugging indoors and storing when the summer is over. The only exception to that are things like the squiggly cane chairs from Hong Kong, which are as light as a feather to carry and can be used as indoor furniture, too.

And unless you are able to leave your garden furniture *in situ* all the time, you don't want anything particularly heavy.

We've all fallen into one or more of these traps in our time, and for lazy people like us, it's sheer disaster. Like that terrible moment when it starts to rain and you remember you've left the swing seat uncovered . . . or those folding chairs that nobody will bother to fold up until their joints have got so stiff that it takes a wrestler to deal with them . . . or the painted furniture that no one will repaint, which eventually rots. Then comes the day of final disaster when that Victorian frivolity of a cast-iron chair, which you picked up at an auction sale, covering its rust with spray paint, disintegrates in a shower of rust as your unfavourite aunt decides to sit on it.

You've three great friends in garden furniture and decoration – plastics, cast aluminium and fibreglass.

At one end of the scale there are plenty of cheap-and-cheerful plastic chairs and tables around now, and if you pick carefully you can find some quite chic ones.

If your way of life, and your purse, afford it, there are marvellous copies of traditional Victorian garden chairs and tables, made in cast aluminium which won't rust. Don't expect them to be cheap, they're not, but they will last for years. Don't expect them to be comfortable, either. Most of them are sheer hell to sit on, bolt upright. But cushions will mitigate the worst, and they are very decorative to look at.

Now fibreglass comes into the market, especially for things like urns and window-boxes, which are unbreakable and long-wearing. They look unbelievably like lead in some versions – you have to touch them to make sure.

Another item that you'll need for your outdoor room is a frame of colourful climbers and shrubs to hide all the household impedimenta ... the bicycle shed, the dustbins and the coal bunkers or the oil tank. So legislate for that, too, in your plan. After all, you'll want to make sure that they are well out of sight and out of mind when you're lying back in the sun, or sitting there watching the sunset and sipping your beer.

Strictly functional

Perhaps your garden is a playground for the children, for the dog – and for the neighbours' children and dogs, too? Then be honest about it, and turn it into one for the time being. But keep an eye on the future. If the children ask you for a paddling pool, buy a flattish fibreglass pond instead, site it carefully and sink it into the ground. Let them paddle in it now, as much as they want, then later, when they've grown up a little, you can stock it with a water-lily and some fish, and hide its nasty edges with paving stones. The same goes for the traditional sand-pit, which is usually shoved at the bottom of the garden. Make it a sand bed instead, somewhere near the house: then, when the children have lost interest in it, you can use it to grow a crop of special sand-loving plants.

If you know that your garden is going to be littered with toys most of the time, make allowances for the fact. Build a shelter of some sort – it could be something you can turn into a carport later on – into which tricycles and toys can be thrust at the end of the day, rather than being carted back into the house and upstairs.

Getting started

Whatever kind of garden you need, first of all you'll have to come to terms with one fact: to get it the way you want it to be, you're going to have to spend some time, or some money, or a mixture of both, if you want a quick effect.

Once you've got it under control, you can let up on both counts. I once inherited a garden that was three-quarters of an acre of neglect. The jungle in Vietnam could not be worse. Trees and bushes were inextricably intertwined, brambles and stinging nettles were everywhere. There was even a splendid patch of mint in the middle of the lawn. I took one look, and hired a local contractor.

'Put it down,' I cried. '*Do* something about it.' He did. He came along with a quartet of splendid, long-haired youths who hacked and chopped and sprayed their way through it, and tidied it up. It cost me forty pounds, but it was well worthwhile. If the garden had been half the size we could have coped. But this was too much.

Your garden is nowhere near that state, I'm sure, but to get it into shape you might think about hiring one or two tools that will help you in the work. The difference that an electric hedge-cutter or motor mower can make, for instance, as compared with the hand-operated variety, might just make it worthwhile to buy one.

You've probably got, or are planning to get, every gadget you can find to make the house easier to run, but don't forget the garden's needs. All lined up to help you – and probably on hire in your local hire shop – are things like flame guns, cultivators, hedge-trimmers and clippers. They'll save you an awful lot of time and labour, and anyway they're much more fun to use.

Save a little money for stocking your garden, though you may be able to cadge plants from neighbours and friends. The planting season stretches over several months from autumn to spring, so you can spread out the expenditure and the work.

Soil sense

Learn to love your soil, just the way it is. You're not going to toil away, digging forkfuls of peat or lime into the ground simply in order to try to grow some plants which don't really want to live there anyway. You're not going to waste time and money, either, in trying to grow on clay things that love sandy soil, or acid-lovers in an alkaline soil. The easiest way to find out what kind of plant flourishes is to ask your next-door neighbour.

What *is* your soil really like? You need to know if you are going to garden the lazy way, for trying to fly in the face of nature takes time *and* effort. So unless you're keen enough, and rich enough, to have all the topsoil removed and replaced by something else, you're lumbered for keeps with what you've already got. If you live on a new estate, you may even have no topsoil at all – though the days when contractors sold the top earth before they sold the house are over. But take a good look, just in case – if *nothing* is trying to grow up through the rubble, be suspicious.

Take a close look at the ground one day when it has

not rained for about 48 hours. Pick up a handful of earth. Is it almost dry? Does it feel light? Does it run in grains between your fingers? Then it is almost certainly sandy in its basic content.

Is it dark and slightly spongy in texture? Does it seem to spring back when you press it? Then you've probably got a soil with a good deal of peat in it.

A chalky soil is pretty obvious even to the uninitiated, from the chalk chips that lurk not far below the surface.

If the ground tends to hold water in puddles, and is inclined to be heavy and treacly, then you're probably the unlucky owner of a clay soil – but cheer up, plenty of plants still love it, you just have to pick the right ones.

Be smart, stick to the kind of plants that will thrive on your own home patch, then half your troubles are over. The people who have gardens in which things don't grow very well, weedy, spindly-looking plants, under-sized trees, are probably planting the wrong things in them. It's as simple as that. And a good deal of the back-breaking, frustrating work that goes on in a garden is caused by this very fact. One quick way to sum up your chances on what you *can* grow is to take a look at any parkland that you have around you, and see what thrives there . . . rhododendrons, silver birches, gorse . . . whatever it is, it will give you a clue or two for your own garden.

Is your soil acid or alkaline? Here's where you have to play chemist – unless you happen to have a hydrangea or two around. Hydrangeas, like litmus paper, have a happy habit of turning pink or blue according to the acidity of the soil. If your hydrangeas are pink, the soil is likely to be alkaline, and if they are purply-blue it is acid – unless of course the previous owner has been monkeying around, adding something to the soil around the plants.

To be sure, test the soil with a special kit you can buy

A chemical soil-testing kit saves a lot of wasted time and effort

from your local horticultural supplier. It can be fun, on a back-to-school basis. Most kits contain a test-tube, some chemical and a colour chart which gives the acidity or alkalinity of the soil, which is measured, like the acid in our skin, by its "pH factor".

You take a small sample of earth and shake it up with the chemical in the tube, then have fun matching its colour against what looks very like a paint chart. If you end up with a high pH number, then your soil is very alkaline, with a great deal of lime in it. If the pH figure is low, then the soil is acid, and likes rhododendrons, azaleas and heathers.

Now some of that mumbo-jumbo in the seedman's catalogue begins to make sense. You have an acid, chalky soil, or a limy, sandy one – now you're getting somewhere. Don't waste time trying to make your garden what it isn't by digging in vast quantities of lime or by adding barrowfuls of peat. If there's something you want to grow *that* much but which is forbidden to you, grow it in a tub, buying the soil for it specially from a local nurseryman. (There's something sneakily satisfactory about beating nature in this way.)

Sum up your enemies, the weeds, like a general going into battle. Talk to your neighbours, find out what the local problem is . . . bindweed, groundsel . . . couch grass . . . or the most dreaded scourge of all, ground elder. They can all be beaten with weed-killer, so don't plan to bend down spending back-breaking hours pulling them out; you've got something better to do with your time. If they haven't taken too much of a hold, you can set other smother plants on them to get them out of the way. (see Chapter 9 for some ideas.)

What do they mean?

Most gardening books assume that you know what they mean when they talk about hardy or half-hardy annuals and so on. But here, for the uninitiated, is a quick run-through on the gardening jargon you might need.

Annuals are plants that flower, seed and die off in one year. You either sow them in seed form or buy them as young plants. Annuals are OUT so far as the lazy gardener is concerned – at least until the garden is so well under control that you can play around with it a little. Annuals are the sort of things that old ladies and small children have great success in growing. But the rest of us may well sow packet after packet of seed which, rather like those instant foods that look so good on the pack, never quite seem to come up to expectations. Birds, slugs and all manner of nasty, creepy-crawly things are partial to the young seedlings of annuals, too. So annuals are not for us. (They have only one advantage over other kinds of plants. They are cheap.)

Even less likely to succeed in the lazy gardener's garden are half-hardy annuals, which need to be started off in trays indoors because otherwise they would be killed off by frost. If annuals are not for us, half-hardy annuals are positive anathema.

Biennials are tiresome plants, especially to us lazy gardeners, because we must have quick results to succeed. Biennials have to be sown one year, but they don't flower until the next. Unfortunately for cottage garden enthusiasts, wallflowers and forget-me-nots come under this category, so we shall have to do without them. It is best to ignore biennials altogether.

Perennial is the magic word for the gardener who wants to cheat, for it's the kind of plant that goes on living for years. A tree is, strictly speaking, a perennial, so is a shrub, but I shall call them by their ordinary names. The hardy herbaceous perennials are our second line of defence in the garden, decorative, colourful flowering plants that will go on for year after year and can be increased, usually, by dividing up the clumps as they grow larger. But even then our whittling down to the lazy man's plants is not finished. We want, as far as possible, to have nothing that needs tying up or staking. If we choose our plants carefully enough we can simply let them sprawl – in many cases we can cheat and pick dwarf varieties, too.

You'll find that I give the correct Latin name-tag for plants I mention in this book. This is a drag, but totally unavoidable. Why? The only way to be sure of getting the right plant is to specify its Latin name to the nurseryman, because what is called "Black-eyed Susan" in one part of the country, may be something quite different elsewhere. Each group of plants, however, has its own Latin family surname, plus the equivalent of a Christian name, which identifies the variety. It's important to give both names to get the right plant.

Take the hellebore family, for instance. It's no use going in and simply asking for a hellebore, because you might get one of several . . . the *Helleborus niger* (Christmas rose) flowers in December but the *Helleborus orientalis* doesn't put in an appearance until late January or February. So when you are ordering plants on any scale you'll have to learn to live with, and love, their pompous Latin names. You just try going into any upper-crust nursery and asking for "Bear's Breeches", for instance;

Climbing plants growing up strings placed to hide an unpleasing view

they'll look at you as if you are mad, since they only know it as *Acanthus*.

What can you do right now, while you're planning? Hide the view from your window, to start with. Beg, borrow or steal a window-box and plant it up with something instant and pretty, to mask some of the view. Or you could do what a friend of mine did, and plant out morning glories and nasturtiums in her window-box and train them up pieces of twine to make a flower curtain, completely blocking the sight of the wilderness beyond.

2
THE GARDEN THAT STARTS FROM SCRATCH

The builders have finally packed up the last of their tools and left. The house is so spick and span, so labour-saving, so new, that you can hardly believe it is really yours.

This euphoria lasts until you look out of the window and survey the rock-strewn wilderness beyond. Everything in the garden is far from lovely.

There are basically two types of builders: The first kind leave everything neat and tidy – and bald. They've levelled up the ground for you, they've carted away the rubbish. But the place looks, somehow, like a prison exercise yard, with not a plant in sight anywhere. The surface is hard-baked and well trodden down – so well trodden that it feels almost like concrete – and any idea of getting a fork or a spade into it seems laughable. A nagging thought begins to come into your mind . . . when they churned the ground over for you, and levelled it with that bulldozer, could they by any chance have been too enthusiastic and put the topsoil underneath? Could you be looking, by any chance, at solid rock?

The second sort of builders are delightfully feckless ones who toss bricks and rubble out at the back with careless abandon, and leave you to sort it all out afterwards. The garden looks as rock-strewn as the north face of the Eiger – and may well slope just as much.

You go out and take a closer look: what meets your tiny eye is fascinating, for it's just like a treasure hunt. There's an old boot or two, some empty Nescafé tins, a dismembered bicycle, perhaps even a bedstead. And it's all yours – including the bindweed that's just beginning to struggle through.

Before you rush off to phone the Council and ask them to cart it all away, take another look at what has been left. That rubble, for instance. Before you part with it, think again. Do you want a terrace outside the back door? Then you may need the bits for a hardcore foundation on which to pour the concrete.

If you've already had a splendid patio built for you, or you're planning to do without one, what about a rock garden? This may well be the best way to take care of that terrible slope down the end, over which you see yourself doing a Cresta Run with the lawn mower. Rubble makes a good base for any sort of rockery, and you can top it up with some prettier stones on the surface, where they will show.

You may have steps or a path in mind. Then the same maxim holds good – you'll need something solid underneath to stop it from sinking, and rubble may be the answer.

Remember too that every slab of stone, every piece of brick you leave in the garden means a few more cubic inches of good solid *something* that the weeds can't get through.

If your garden has been left bald, then there's nothing to do but organise the digging. If it is rubbish-strewn, then make a glorious bonfire of the branches, old boxes, etc. Children (your own or someone else's) are very good at bonfires – under supervision – and will usually collect rubbish enthusiastically in return for being able to dance round the flames or cook baked potatoes in the ashes. Get them to help cart the rubble, too. Then spread the ashes, spray the ground with weed-killer (see Chapter 7) and leave the land fallow while you plan your future moves.

First things first

Which way does your garden face? That's the next question. Make a note of which areas are most likely to get lots of sun and which will stay in the shade; which walls are exposed to prevailing wind and weather, and which might provide shelter for more exotic plants.

Is your garden basically dark and shady, or open and windy? On many new estates the wind whistles unmercifully over the chain-link fences and the barren ground, making you feel, when you stand in the middle of your patch, like a character from a Brontë novel.

You don't want to waste time slogging away on plants that don't want to live with *you*, coaxing limp little leaves to perk up and grow. So you're going to pick the kind of shrubs and plants that like your soil. But you need to know whether they like sun or shade, too, so bear that in mind when you come to order them.

Don't think of your garden in one dimension only. It's a stage set, basically. And just as a good stage designer can hoodwink the audience into thinking that what they are looking at is larger and more lavish than it really is, so you too with very little effort can kid everyone into thinking that you've a superb garden by using the same tricks.

But the trouble is that most people are still stuck somewhere *circa* 1902 in their garden thinking, and plan their plot like a municipal park, with regimented flower beds ranged round the outside, a rectangle of bald-looking lawn in the centre. And they pick plants that need endless cossetting. But *you* are going to stick mainly to trees and shrubs.

First let's get rid of a few fallacies. Why have the flower beds round the edge? Most people treat their garden as though they were clearing it as an auditorium for a giant outdoor rally. The reason for this is a complete mystery to me. If you want to run an open-air discothèque, or lay out a clock golf course, or a karting track, fine; otherwise, why make more work for yourself by stowing back against the fence the very things that will make useful landscapers or screens?

Loosen up your ideas on garden planning, learn to live without straight lines. (But don't go mad, on the other hand, as my mother's gardener once did: he carved her lawn into the shape of a violin – we never knew quite why. The result was that every time we tried to mow it, we had to do so in great drunken sweeps.)

Stand in the middle of the ground and look in each direction. Decide first where the utility things like dustbins, sheds, rubbish heaps, will go. Then think again about that terrace. Do you really *want* one at the back of the house? Will it get the sun? Might it not be better to put it somewhere else?

The practical application of a chunk of concrete behind the back door is that it gets rid of the worst of the muddy feet problem. But if it happens to face north, if you're not going to get any sunshine on you when you want to sit and relax on it, perhaps it would be better to keep it to a narrow strip and have the real terrace somewhere different – at the end of the garden, for instance, where you can relax out of sight and sound of the house.

You may have inherited a ready-made patio, of course, but if it is of no use where it is, it might be to your advantage to roof it in and use it as an outdoor/indoor room.

Display flower beds are another thing. Have you thought of having them in the centre of the garden, with the grass round the outside? There's no reason why they shouldn't be placed that way. A tree set well in from the boundary wall, too, will look much more attractive than tucked away in the corner. You can appreciate its shape more, and it may obligingly hide something unsightly set behind it. The arrangement has another advantage, too – you'll avoid all those arguments with neighbours over roots undermining their fence, or boughs overhanging it, and if the tree has any fruit on it, it'll be all your own.

People seem to be frightened of buying trees, somehow. They don't realise that you can quite easily get them already grown to a respectable height, and that even small ones will shoot up quickly to a viable size. There is one well-known specialist nursery, Hilliers of Winchester, who will sell you trees as tall as 20 feet high – at a price. So remember that it might well pay you to buy a tree or two instead of concentrating on flower beds. You can then cluster one or two dwarf shrubs around the tree or plant bulbs under it, in the grass.

Pick an evergreen tree, by the way, or you'll spend your autumn gazing disconsolately at the leaves strewn all over the grass, and who wants to spend spare time raking up leaves? A cypress, for instance, looks splendid standing by itself and has a nice tall but compact shape. *Chamaecyparis lawsoniana* grows fast, and several in a row can be used as a hedge or screen; *Cupressocyparis leylandii* grows even faster.

Planning with a purpose

Use your planting to alter the *apparent* shape of your garden, if what you've got has unfortunate proportions. A short, wide garden can be made to look longer if you plant a row of trees or bushes at the bottom, a foot or two in front of the fence but stopping short of the boundaries on either side. Leave a gap in the centre, and it gives the impression from the house that your garden goes on beyond the greenery.

The long, thin garden, a suburban curse, can be made to look wider if you use the stage-set principle of split-

A long, narrow garden can be made to look wider

ting it up into a series of separate "rooms". I once had a garden so narrow that it was virtually nothing but a footpath to what had been a privy at the end. It could best be described as a real challenge. But by placing beds of shrubs at right-angles to the fence on alternate sides at a time, I made it look both shorter and wider than it really was.

Most people make the classic mistake of turning a long, narrow plot into something even narrower and longer by bisecting it bang down the middle with a path.

You need something to walk on, of course, but instead of a path have stepping stones scattered on the grass. Here's how you lay them: place the stone on the lawn where you want it to be, trace round it with a sharp garden knife, then cut out a piece of turf to accommodate it accordingly. It is only the matter of a minute or so's work – if you simply tread it into the grass you'll have extra trouble for evermore mowing round it, for otherwise the mower blades will come into a collision course with the concrete and get blunted or worse still, spat out. When laying stepping stones it pays to be realistic and find out first where people are liable to walk. Human beings have an irritating habit of not always doing what you hope they will do.

If you *must* have a proper path, set it to one side and make it meander a little round those beds by the fence. Anything but right down the middle is the motto.

Make the framework, the basic bones of your garden, a series of evergreens, particularly if you have ugly boundary fencing to hide. But you don't have to stick to trees: there are plenty of shrubs that will do the job just as well, especially in a small garden – rhododendrons, for instance, if they will grow in your soil; they're good-looking all the year round, with their glossy dark leaves. Holly is another useful quick-grower that has a practical use, too, around Christmas time – provided you get one of the right sex.

Use dark greens like these for the back row and pick lighter shades of green as you move towards the centre. This simple trick, used by artists, will help to make your garden look larger than it really is. Then between the greens, space in here and there the shrubs that you're picking for their colour . . . those that turn a fiery red in the autumn, those that have fantastic flowers. Reserve for spots near the house the special shrubs that give you colour in winter – you're unlikely to want to wander outside, but it's nice to see them near the window. Don't think in terms of flowers alone – many plants have interesting leaves.

If you're keen on roses, *don't* have a special rose bed, for nothing looks more bleak and barren in winter. Mix them up instead among the other plants. The same goes for anything that has one brief season of colour, and anything that sheds its leaves. While your neighbours' gardens look gloomy, dripping and dank, yours can still be colourful if you plan properly. You'll find some ideas in chapter 9.

Ignore the Weary Willies who tell you to space your shrubs well apart when you plant them. You don't want the place to look like a cemetery, do you? Don't sit back and wait for the shrubs to grow into the gaps provided for them, crowd them together at first to get a good instant effect. You're going to have to divide some of them anyway, as they get bigger, and many plants love a change of scene from time to time. Rhododendrons, for instance, positively thrive on being shoved around from one corner to another, it actually stimulates their growth. They're nice and easy to shift, too, because they are so shallow-rooted. I have some that have been moved from several houses in turn, and that still get carted around in my present garden. Remember, as a conscientious cheat, you are planting for *now*, not for later.

When it comes to planning for herbaceous plants and

flowers, remember this simple rule – if it has a dwarf variety, that's the one you buy. And this goes particularly for bushy, unwieldy things like Michaelmas daisies. That way you have little or no staking to do. After all, who wants to spend all summer propping things up, or tying them down?

Getting the hard graft done

You're ready to go? Beg, borrow or steal a cultivator first, to turn over the soil. It's by far the easiest way out. But unless you're planning to do a lot of future garden work, you certainly won't want to *buy* a machine. Most suburbs now have a hire shop which can lend you one for the weekend – and other useful tools, too. Get to know it. If you're unlucky and don't have such a shop in your area, put an advertisement in your local paper: there's sure to be a keen gardener somewhere who's feeling rather guilty over all the money he's spent on his machine and who will lend it to you for a few bob a day. That way it will help earn its keep.

Cultivators usually fit happily into estate cars or in Dormobiles; I have even towed one slowly behind a Mini. See Chapter 6 for details about the different types available. Use the machine to churn up all areas of the garden that are to be planted. (But don't dig up the strips where there are to be paths, terraces or sheds.) Pick a day when the soil is reasonably moist but it doesn't look like rain. If you're unlucky enough to choose bad weather, you may end up with a quagmire on your hands, and a machine to hose down.

Cultivators are *fun* – at first. They will turn over the ground in rough ridges, rather like mini-ploughs. Use yours to mark out the garden as you go – up and down one way for where the lawn will be, round and round in the shape of beds for shrubs or trees. That's the easiest way to plan your plot without any of that nonsense with wooden pegs and string.

Get the paths and the terrace sorted out first of all. Then you'll have something to walk on and to wheel barrows over, if necessary. Now comes the time when you could cut corners with professional help. But if you are short of cash don't use "official" garden contractors. Look out for moon-lighters instead. They're builders' labourers, council workers and so on who are often glad to earn spare-time money doing this sort of work.

We once found a splendid fireman who was also a car mechanic, a plumber and a gardener off duty, and since he was on shiftwork he was able to put in a lot of odd hours during the day. But don't go marching up to your local Fire Station and enquire – the men are not officially supposed to have any spare-time businesses. Put an advertisement in the local paper, or a card in the window of the newsagent's shop, ask around. You're sure to find someone.

My brother-in-law once had a very nasty concrete path that he was longing to be rid of. He'd bounced up and down it with sledgehammers for weeks, even tried attacking it with an electric drill without making the slightest dent in its surface. Then one day he noticed a gang of road contractors working nearby, and asked the foreman if he could do anything about the path for him. A giant Irishman came along, and stared down at the concrete path. He went away and fetched a pickaxe. One blow and the entire path was shattered into crazy paving which was swiftly carted away in their lorry. The price? The cost of beers all round.

A friend who got tired of tending the grass in his small back garden had the entire thing covered with paving for less than a quarter of a contractor's quoted price by a carpenter who did gardening in his spare time. It all goes to show that it is worthwhile enquiring outside about help, and not accepting the first tender you receive.

There's no doubt, though, that the cheapest way of

You can usually find the right man for the job if you look around

all to build a path or a terrace is to do it yourself with paving slabs or ready-mixed concrete. The work involved means a nasty weekend, but once it is done, you are freed from chores in that part of the garden forever. It might even pay you, if you have a small enough garden to make the idea possible, to cover almost all of it with concrete paving stones, doing it in three sections at three different levels, and completing each as you have the cash available. With the addition of plant troughs, shrubs growing in pots and the odd tree or two, it's the ideal lazy gardener's garden. But the initial work and costs you come up against are not small.

Here's how you build a terrace: Be a cheat, organise a garden(ing) party for your youngest, healthiest friends. Promise them unlimited food and wine or beer while they help you with the building work. The age of chivalry is not completely dead, and there is usually a supply of strong young men on tap who haven't yet got involved with gardening on their own home ground and don't realise yet what hard work it is. Look out, too, for the frustrated gardener, the flat-dweller who longs for a plot of ground of his own, and meanwhile would love to give you a hand with yours. I even know of one man who takes part of his summer holiday doing gardening for a friend. I can't promise you'll find someone like him, but it's worthwhile trying. Rope them all in to help you – you'll need them.

First decide the height that the terrace is going to be and whether you will need a foundation to build it on, to bring it up to back-door level. (But make sure that the terrace will come *below* the damp-course level of your house, for you don't want problems with mildewy walls.)

The best-looking terrace is the one that is made from slabs of hand-cut York stone. This is not for us. Neither, probably, is the one that is made from old paving slabs sold off by the local Council. I have yet to find a town

Council that has any left. They've become a myth, like those old gas-lamps you were supposed to find in scrap yards for a few shillings.

You are most certainly stuck with a patio made from pre-cast concrete blocks, but you can get them now in a lot of different un-concrety shades, and match them up too with a retaining wall in the same colour.

Measure the amount of ground to be covered. Do your sums and order your materials. You will need enough slabs to cover the area, plus one or two over in case of accidents. You will need also, apart from any rubble, a quantity of sand that is enough to make a layer about 2 inches thick all over the patio area. You will then need extra sand, or sand and cement, to go between the slabs, depending on the method you choose to fill the gaps.

Level the surface of the ground or the hardcore. Tread it as flat as you can, rather as though you were stamping on the grapes at vintage-time; better still, borrow a garden roller to do the job.

Now spread a layer of sand over the foundation, 3

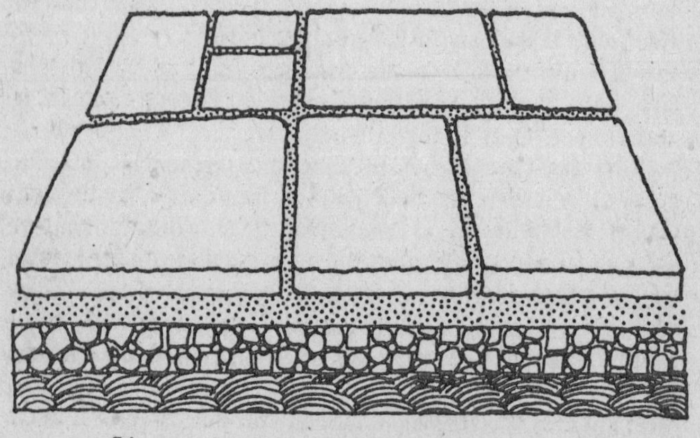

Diagram showing method of laying paving stones

inches deep alongside the house, tapering off to only 1 inch deep at the garden side. This sounds like an almost non-existent slope, but it will make a dickens of a difference when the rains come, for the water will run away from your back door instead of into it. So organise the sand so that it slopes slightly.

Now lay the paving slabs carefully on top, making sure that they line up with the wall of the house. Leave ½ inch between them, all round, for the filling. Each slab must lie flat crosswise, and slope slightly away from the house, sitting comfortably in the sand. Tap the slab with the wrong side of a mallet, to make sure it is lying snugly and doesn't rock. Use a spirit level to check all is well.

Fill the gaps in between the slabs with pure sand if you're planning to plant it with creeping, crawling things for a rustic look, or seal up the stones with a mixture of 2 parts sand and 1 part cement, just slightly moistened to make a mortar. Use the edge of a plank of wood the thickness of the gap to wedge the mixture down firmly. Leave your terrace for at least 24 hours to set before attempting to walk on it. If it's your only way to and from the dustbins, legislate for this by building a cat-walk of a plank perched on bricks.

If you've built your terrace above garden level it will need finishing off with something. The most decorative and easy way of doing this is to make a low screen of pierced concrete blocks. They're child's play to put together, but they cost more than bricks. Don't forget your drains, incidentally. If you need some curiously shaped slabs to fit round them, first take a pattern of the shape with a piece of lino and mark it out on the stone. Then etch it in sharply with a chisel. One hefty tap, with a hammer, and the correct-shaped piece of stone should fall out.

The cheapest terrace of all is the one that is laid in concrete. It's the best, too, in many ways, because once it's in place, nothing should be able to grow through it – the snag about paving stones. If you're game enough to do your own concreting, choose the ready-mixed variety to save time, and lay it 5 inches deep on a ready-prepared bed of rubble and aggregate. No one wants to have to gaze out on a sea of greyish-white, so mix in a colouring agent to give it a yellowish or pinkish hue. Give your patio some surface interest, don't leave it plain. The time to do this is about an hour after the concrete has been slapped down and levelled off. You can drag a piece of wet sacking over it carefully, to give it a non-slip surface and a suitably aged appearance, or you can even fake the look of paving slabs, with a little guile. Here's the method:

Take a shortish piece of planking, one you can handle, and about ¾ inch thick. Using the side for the purpose, carefully score the still-damp concrete into squares. This needs crafty lining up beforehand with chalk marks put as guides on the wall of the house and sticks hammered into the ground at the other end. Use the plank to make a deep score, but make sure that it doesn't go all the way down to the sand underneath. If you have a really large area to mark, or will have difficulty in reaching the centre of the terrace, you're better off getting a squared-up framework of battening made up for you first. Put it down before you pour the concrete. You'll find you can lift it out afterwards without much difficulty.

A pebbled look is another good way oı making ordinary concrete look prettier. Where to get the pebbles? well, there's always the beach . . . Lay your base of cement, leaving about another 2 inches or so to go to bring it up to the right height. Now mix up more cement with the pebbles and spread it over, like icing on a cake. When the concrete has really set properly – it's best to wait about a week in wet weather – you can hose the terrace down and polish odd particles off the stones.

Now for the planting

Your terrace is done. The pros and cons of grass, and how to lay it, are dealt with in Chapter 4. So let's deal with planting time. You're looking for trouble-free trees and shrubs to begin with, plus some herbaceous flowers and bulbs which will look after themselves. You can choose them from the list at the end of this chapter, and you'll find other ideas further on.

First make your master list. Even though few of us can afford to go out cheque book in hand, and stock up the garden then and there, it's important to work out what you intend to buy and to make sure you buy it from the right place.

Don't be tempted to purchase the odd potted plant you see stuck out on the pavement in the High Street. Its chances of survival in your hands are not too good. Buy the best quality plants you can afford, even if it means fewer of them. After all, you don't want to run a convalescent home, do you? Then don't buy anything that needs careful nursing.

It goes without saying that if you want geraniums, fuchsias, roses, clematis or any other well-known plants, it's well worthwhile going to a firm that specialises in them. You can easily find them from advertisements in Sunday papers and in the gardening magazines. When you order from a specialist, pick his brains unashamedly, find out exactly how to plant the things, where they are happiest. After all, he wants you to come back for more, so he's bound to be helpful.

Plan your planting between October and March, buying a few specimens each week. That way the actual chore of planting is made lighter, and the strain is easier on your purse.

However, nobody but a madman – and certainly not one of us indolent gardeners – would dream of putting in plants, shrubs or trees when the frost has turned the ground into a Macadam road, or when it is so soggy underfoot that Wellington boots sink in the soil up to their tops. But, luck being the way it is, the chances are that *your* little parcel of goodies will arrive in the middle of just such weather.

Don't panic. Leave them in a coolish place like a garage for a few days, their roots encased in a plastic bag to keep in the moisture (the nurseryman may well have done that for you already). They'll be perfectly happy for a while.

If the weather is all right, though, but that marvellous display bed you were going to dig strategically right in front of the dustbins hasn't been finished yet, simply hack out a rough trench somewhere and plant your shrubs temporarily in that. If you make sure that plenty of soil is firmed down over their roots they'll stay like that indefinitely without harm, certainly for a week or so, by when, we hope, their new home will be ready. (This is what the professionals call "heeling in".)

If you've got a nasty, mean, thin-looking kind of soil, the sort that looks crumbly and grey and unhealthy, give it a tonic before putting in your plants. Buy some farm straw (you can get it from most pet shops), soak it well with a hose for an hour or so, or leave it out in the weather until it begins to rot, then put a handful in the hole you dig for each of your plants. It will give them a good start in life.

Don't believe in all this business of making out plans for your planting positions on graph paper. If the plants are of a reasonable size, there's only one way to treat them: like furniture. Put them down where you plan to plant them, prop them up, stand back and take a look. It's the only way to decide if they're right where they are.

Always dig a hole wide enough for the roots to spread out and breathe properly, but never dig one too deep, or the poor plant will be desperately groping down towards Australia to find something to feed from. Most

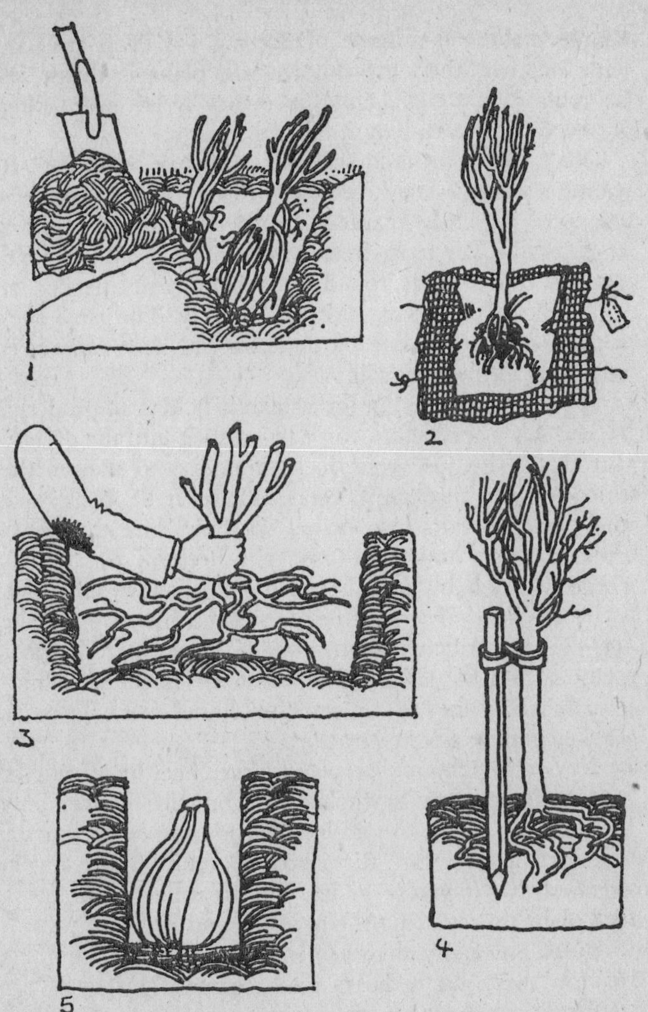

Planting reminders: 1. Heel in plants if you can't deal with them at once. 2. Remove packing materials from roots before planting. 3. Give the roots enough room to lie naturally. 4. If a stake is needed, set it in before putting in the plant. 5. Bulbs need to be sat firmly on the earth, with no pocket of air underneath them

people make the mistake of digging too deep and not wide enough, then the unfortunate plant is thrust in, its roots in a tangle, and the owner is left wondering for ever afterwards why it looks so poorly.

Don't forget to undo the plant from its wrapping. It sounds obvious, I know, but I've heard of at least one person who regularly planted shrubs still in their plastic bags. Shake the roots free, hold the plant upright and draw a rough circle round it. If it's already packed in a ball of soil, however, leave it that way. The same goes if it is encased in one of those special new containers which rot away in the soil.

If your plant cries out for a stake to hold it up properly, *take it out again* before you drive a stick into the ground – it would be just your luck otherwise to skewer the thing straight through its roots. Whatever happens, once the plant is in its new home, do make sure the soil is pressed firmly round it – use your heel for the job. A shrub, like a baby, feels insecure unless it is tightly held.

By the way, if when the time comes for planting the weather is a trifle on the nippy side, don't leave the poor plant out on the lawn while you stomp in for your Sunday lunch. Fling an old coat or a sack over its roots, or they may be affected by the cold.

If you're planning to plant large, healthy shrubs or trees, why prepare a whole bed for them? You're only inviting the weeds to join in. Instead, simply lift out the relevant piece of turf, dig a hole of the right size, put in some straw, if you're giving this treatment, and plonk the plant in, replacing the grass around it.

Bulbs are fiddly things to plant, and if you are going in for them on a large scale, especially if you are naturalising them in grass, it's worthwhile buying a special bulb planter, a tool that will make a nice, neat, rectangular hole in which the bulb will happily sit. The trouble with pointed things like dibbers, which are usually used for the job, is that they leave a narrow triangle of nothing under the base of the bulb, which then has difficulty in getting at any nourishment with its root fibres. Bulbs like to sit *on* something, and who can blame them?

Trees and shrubs

A pleasant mixture of trees and shrubs makes for the laziest garden of the lot, because they need so little attention and, unlike the rest of us, grow more lovely with the years.

Trees must be kept in scale – you don't want to find you've planted a monster in your midst – and for the average suburban garden it's a case of sticking to the small ornamental trees like the flowering almond or flowering cherry. The *Prunus* family to which they both belong has tended to become a bore from over-exposure; but for sheer showy display in early spring, the Japanese ornamental cherry can't be beaten. It's just right if you don't mind keeping up with the Joneses whether you like it or not – because they're bound to have one, too. Another obliging set of trees are the Japanese maples, the *Acer* family. If you've plenty of space, though, plant instead the Norwegian maple; it's a good sharp grower and has crowds of yellow flowers, with bright green leaves which follow suit and themselves turn yellow in autumn.

As a child I planted a sycamore seed-pod right outside the back door of our house. When we moved away, nine years later, it was becoming quite a problem – by now, I should think, it has uprooted the house, for the sycamore is one of the fastest growers of the lot. This also comes from the maple family, by the way, though you might not guess by looking.

The *Robinias*, the false acacias, are very pretty and grow up quickly. Try *Robinia pseudoacacia* (sometimes unfairly called the "Black Locust", heaven knows why). It thrives anywhere, even in town, and has pretty white flowers. *Robinia hispida* is the rose acacia, with clusters of pink flowers in summer.

If you've got a pond and you're determined to plant a weeping willow, don't choose the standard variety, or it will weep over the whole of your garden, since it grows to 20 feet or more. The kind you want is *Salix caprea pendula* or *Salix purpurea* "Pendula", both small trees that will stop growing at about 8 feet in height. Another pretty little tree is the weeping version of the Cotoneaster – *Cotoneaster x hybridus* "Pendulus", which has evergreen glossy leaves and red berrries in a shower-like form.

You don't need a computer dating system to tell whether you and a particular shrub of your choice are well suited or not – it's simply a matter of commonsense. So here, for the record, is a run-down of some of the better-known garden shrubs listed under special conditions which they can tolerate:

For Chalky Soils

Berberis: the Barberry plant, with masses of yellow-orange flowers and red berries.
Buddleia: A shrub with distinctive flower spikes of purple-red, mauve, lilac or white.
Cotoneaster: Foliage varies from dark and glossy to matt and hairy; berries may be black, purple-red, orange-red apricot, yellow, etc.
Crataegus: The hawthorn family, with pink or crimson flowers.
Forsythia: With yellow sprays of flowers in spring.
Helianthemum: The sun rose, a tiny shrub suitable for rock gardens.
Hypericum: Rose of Sharon, a low-growing shrub with yellow flowers.
Philadelphus: The mock orange, a delicate-looking bush with white flowers.
Prunus: Flowering almonds, apricots, cherries, etc.

Ribes: The flowering currant family – can be grown as a hedge.
Spartium: Spanish broom, inclined to be straggly, with yellow flowers.
Spiraea: Graceful arching stems, flower sprays of pink or white.
Syringa: The true lilac, with scented flower sprays.

For Lime-free Soils

Andromeda: A member of the heather and heath family; has bright pink flowers.
Azalea: One division of the rhododendron family (see below); good for small gardens; very lovely colours.
Daphne: An old-fashioned shrub with sprays of close-packed pink, white or green flowers.
Erica: The heathers, usually with pink flowers.
Kalmia: Has clusters of pink flowers that look rather like hydrangeas.
Magnolia: A magnificent shrub/tree.
Pieris: An interesting shrub – in some species the tips of the branches sport bright red leaves in spring, and later there are sprays of white flowers.
Rhododendron: Although this shrub will grow elsewhere, it prefers a lime-free soil; there are dozens of varieties and colours to choose from.

For Clay Soils

Cornus: The dogwood, with yellow flowers and berries of red, blue, black or white.
Deutzia: An obliging shrub, with white or pink single or double flowers.
Diervilla: A North American shrub with bright yellow flowers.
Escallonia: A shrub that likes the sea-side; it has sprays of deep pink/red flowers.
Genista: Broom, with sprays of sweet-pea-shaped flowers in yellow.

Lonicera: Our old friend the honeysuckle; pick an evergreen version.
Pyracantha: The firethorn; can be trained up a wall; has dark green leaves and red, orange or yellow berries.
Rubus: The bramble – has pretty but untidy white or pink flowers like wild roses.
Rosa: All roses will grow happily on clay soil, but be different – go for the old-fashioned varieties.
Viburnum: A good old standard suburban shrub with white flowers – in one or two species these are borne in ball-like clusters.
Also suitable for Clay: Berberis, Buddlèia, Cotoneaster, Crataegus, Forsythia, Hypericum, Philadelphus, Prunus, Ribes, Spiraea and *Syringa* – see notes above.

For Poor or Sandy Soils

Cistus: Rock roses; small and hardy, with pinkish-crimson, pink or white flowers.
Cytisus: Broom: (related to the brooms mentioned above, whose Latin name is *Genista*); most species have lavish sprays of yellow flowers.
Lavendula: Old English lavender – it blends well with roses.
Rosa spinosissima: A form of rose that thrives in poor soils.
Rosmarinus: A herb, strictly speaking – rosemary, the aromatic shrub.
Ulex: Ugly name for a pretty shrub – gorse, with its yellow flowers.
And also: Berberis, Crataegus, Cotoneaster, Helianthemum – see above.

3
THE OLDER GARDEN

Taking over an old garden that has been planned and cared for by someone else is rather like acquiring a mother-in-law. It's probably not what you would have chosen, but you're stuck because you wanted what went with it. It's set in its ways, and there's not much you can change except by coaxing and craftiness.

But if there is one thing worse than inheriting a grandiose Victorian plot, the kind with formal flower beds and urns, it is taking over a *piece* of an old estate – something that happens quite often now if you buy part of an old house, or have a new bungalow built in the grounds.

Our garden is like that. It has an imposing flight of urn-decked steps that leads absolutely nowhere – or, to be more precise, leads straight to the length of chain-link fence which divides us off from our neighbour (he has the old kitchen garden). However, we're lucky. It's not possible to see what a fraud the offending steps are, because there's a shrubbery that hides the view beyond. But many unlucky owners find themselves the proud possessors of a path that leads straight into a high fence, or even, as I heard in one case, of *half* a lily-pond. The man with the path solved his problem in an unusual way: He put a large mirror at the end of it, and surrounded it by evergreen creepers growing on battens. The garden now seems to stretch ahead indefinitely.

There may be more than fairies at the bottom of your garden – there may be a greenhouse. Don't be too hasty

Don't be too hasty in getting rid of an old conservatory or summer-house – you may be able to convert it into something attractive

and get rid of it. It might come in useful. You can always paint over the glass and turn it into a garden shed, for instance. If it's sited in a pleasant position, though, you could turn it into a summer house for yourself. Give the outside a coat of paint, whitewash the roof panes if it lets in too much light and heat, even install venetian blinds on some of the side windows, and you're ready to go. Clear out those shelves and staging for plants. Put in their place a deckchair, a transistor radio and one or two scented pot plants that are easy to look after (see Chapter 12); you could even build a bar. Then when it is sunny but windy you can view the rest of the world from your glass-house.

Some old houses have a battered conservatory clinging like a limpet to their side. Don't be in a hurry to get rid of this, either, if it is structurally sound. You can always use it as a bicycle store and a place to put all those things like tennis rackets, footballs, ice-skates and so on which take up so much room. A conservatory is wonderful in summer as a studio or a sewing-room, because there's so much light. If it is conveniently near the kitchen, you could plant a quick-growing vine, train it under the roof and install a small barbecue for eating *al fresco*.

The Victorian garden usually has flower beds, dozens of them, with *things* growing in them, stiffly staked. But the chances are that you'll take it over at just the time of the year when it's virtually impossible to know what those sodden, greyish spikes actually represent.

So here's maxim number one about old gardens – and one which we'll all heartily endorse: *do absolutely nothing at first*. Wait and see what you've got growing there. Don't rush in and rip out everything – you're probably doing that to the house, anyway. I know a lady who tore out what appeared to be a particularly ugly bush and burned it, only to find out afterwards that it was some myrtle grown from a sprig that had been used in Queen Victoria's wedding bouquet.

So if you move in during the autumn, just let it all lie fallow. You may be in for some pleasant surprises. Hang on until spring, when bulbs may appear magically in just the patch you were thinking about digging up. Apparently-dead trees may break into bud. You may find, too, that there's a *reason* for that awful-looking mass of bristly branches by the back door; they could be an early-flowering shrub. Even if a tree does turn out to be dead, or extremely unpleasant looking, don't think you've got to pull it out – use it as a prop to grow climbers like wistaria or clematis.

Down with bedding out

Of course, your garden is bound to need a re-think eventually. After all, you're not going to spend *your* summer planting out regiments of geraniums – the mainstay of Victorian flower-beds. So the first thing to do is to attack the flower-bed problem right away, before the weeds get a look in.

Unless the garden is minute, start from the fence inwards and pack in all the quick-growing shrubs that you can afford, among any others that are already there. Reduce the number of flower beds you have to look after – plan to grass some over – and move the occupants to help crowd out the others. Most Victorian flower beds are far too deep from front to back, so make them narrower, encourage the grass to grow over them in front, shift any useful-looking clumps of flowers further back. That way you'll end up, eventually, with a narrow band of shrubs and a few flowers that can look after themselves, things that are easy to push the mower around and need no attention. A garden of this type is bound to have lavish areas of lawn, so if grass-cutting is going to be *the* chore, keep the flower beds as small as possible.

If the beds are very wide, especially if they are alongside the lawn, it might pay you to buy some turf right away and lay it in a line inside the edge. It's easy to do – for details see Chapter 4. By doing this you'll get a quick effect and keep the weeds under. But check first of all that there are no nasty tinny edgings in the soil, designed to keep the lawn at bay. If there are, root them out, or they'll play havoc with your mower blades.

A neglected garden, one that hasn't been touched for a year or so, needs tougher tactics. In some cases, you can't even see what form it was supposed to take in the first place. Then the only thing to do is to hire a rotary scythe and hack down the nettles and the couch grass so that you can see what's underneath. Don't be tempted to tackle it by hand. But if this is quite unavoidable, use a sickle, and remember the tip given to me by an old countryman: keep the hand that is not holding the

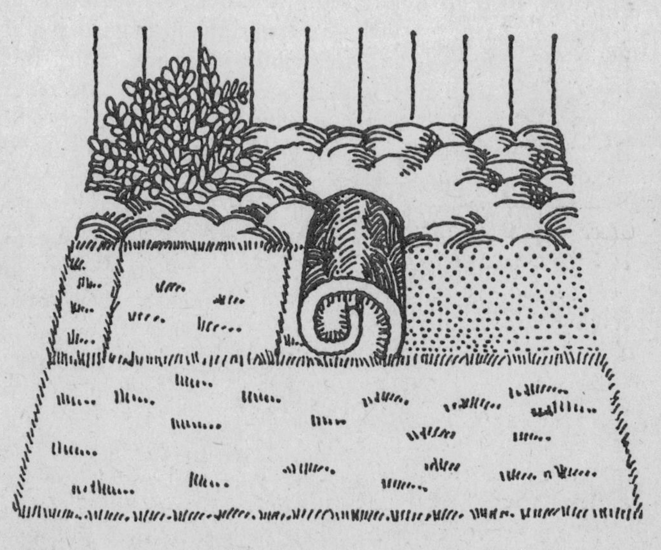

Flower border too wide? You can narrow it by laying turves

sickle firmly resting on your knee – never let it simply hang by your side, or you may look down and find you've sliced it off.

Rule number two for old gardens: don't pull anything out unless you have something else to put in its place – otherwise you're positively inviting the ground elder to move in.

Deletions and additions

It takes a full year to find out exactly what *is* going on in your garden. You never know what strange treasures may be lurking there. But the time arrives when you've got to take stock of the existing shrubs and plants and to get in others that will blend in with their surroundings. Let's think about a few of the classic old suburban things you may find, and those you might like to import.

Box Edging was one of the Victorians' great loves. It appealed to their innate sense of order. They grew it in miniature mazes everywhere – round the herb garden and the kitchen garden and frequently alongside paths. But the trouble with box is that over the years it becomes extremely thin and scruffy-looking around the base, and the only way to make it look good is to trim it regularly – which is not on the lazy gardener's social calendar.

If you do plan to keep it, buy some secateurs, ruthlessly clip off all the dead wood, then cut the box down to about a foot above the ground. It should then make fresh good growth the next year and become a respectable hedge.

If you decide to pull it out, you're in for a surprise: pulling box out of the ground is like extracting an elephant's tusk – extremely difficult to do. It's tenacious and its roots go a long, long way. In our garden we were able to use a rope and a Land-Rover to get the worst out – you may not be so lucky. If you want to get rid of the hedge effect, but begin to flag after the first tussle or two, try taking out every other piece of box, and clipping the rest into the shape of small bushes. If not, learn to love it and live with it.

The Laburnum is what I call a suburban tree. In some places there is one in every garden, tucked away by the fence. There is nothing particularly wrong with it, the only problem is that familiarity breeds contempt. If yours is a small one, you could move it to a place by itself. Most laburnum trees have a surprisingly pretty shape about them, particularly the one called "Golden Rain", and splendid flower showers, too. Laburnums don't live particularly long, but if a tree becomes unwieldy you can always cut it down to size in winter by lopping off the larger branches and shortening others.

Witch Hazel is a shrub to buy if you haven't already got one in the garden, because it obligingly flowers in winter – it is just like having an after-Christmas present to see the first feathery flowers appear on its twiggy branches early in January – they're like stars. Witch hazel is a big, bushy plant that can grow 12 feet high unless you cut it back after flowering, so put it somewhere where it can grow unchecked. If yellow is not your colour – and its surprising just how many winter flowers are yellow – ask for the variety called "Carmine Red". Witch hazel's official name is *Hamamelis* and the common yellow kind, which is also the most vigorous grower of the lot, is called *Hamamelis mollis.*

Hydrangeas were an obligatory part of any Victorian garden, but anyone who actually goes out and *buys* the common kind needs her head examined. Not only is it one of the nastiest-looking flowering plants I know (*chacune à son goût*) but almost everyone has some in the garden and it is easy to propagate, if you keep the cuttings in the warm.

But if you are trying to fill up a gap in your garden quickly, hydrangeas come in very handy indeed. They're happy anywhere in the sun or partial shade and they love a drink. I have a huge bush of them growing in a rather sour part of the garden right next to a drain pipe which frequently overflows. They love it there.

Hydrangeas are meant to shoot up as much as 6 feet high, so if yours shows signs of this sort of growth, don't panic and take a machete to it. Think: if you chop off the top it will burgeon sideways instead. The kind that you've probably inherited is the *Hydrangea Macrophylla*, the one with huge ball-like clusters of flowers. It's a great pity, when there are so many more interesting varieties of hydrangea available, that most of us end up with the good old common pink. There's the lace-cap kind, for instance, which has pretty starry flowers and flat tops, and which looks rather like giant cow-parsley viewed from the distance. Another type that no one seems to know much about is the climbing *Hydrangea petiolaris*, which will clamber happily up walls and fences, even over trees, as long as it has plenty of moisture. Even the dark red version of the common Hydrangea looks like a totally different flower. I once saw some growing in the back garden of a row of railwaymen's cottages, and almost fell out of the train when I realised what it was. It must have been a variety called "Westfalen".

Bamboos and *Pampas Grasses* are beastly if they are left in a corner of the garden. But take the pampas, for instance, and put it in a circular bed by itself and it becomes a very splendid sight indeed, with giant feathery fronds that last well into the winter. The Victorians used them for decoration indoors. They can make a splendid decoration for your lawn instead – and they look good all the year round.

Forsythia is a good old standby shrub, but in my garden at any rate the birds seem to think it has been planted as a free picnic, and attack the young flower-buds. Forsythia's greeny-yallery flowers shoot out like golden rain fireworks early in the spring, when the garden could do with some colour. But it's inclined to look unattractive when it's not actually in flower, so if you have inherited some in a very prominent position, it might be an idea to re-site it in a corner. If you are planning to buy a new forsythia plant, either go for a very tall variety like "Lynwood", which will shoot up 8 feet or more and can be shoved back against a fence, or try the dwarf version, "Arnold", which spreads sideways and crouches obligingly only 2 feet or so high.

Fuchsias are often looked on only as greenhouse plants, which is a shame, because they're so showy and so easy to look after if you choose the hardy outdoor variety – any of the Magellanica family, for instance. I once saw a little low hedge of fuchsias in a suburban front garden and it looked very pretty; it was probably the variety known as "Tom Thumb", which has violet petals and rose-pink sepals to its flowers. Don't worry if your fuchsias appear to have died off or disappeared altogether after a sharp frost – they will revive miraculously when the warmer weather comes. If you want to be kind to them, and to be rewarded with stronger growth, plant them in a warm sheltered place (notice next time you have heavy frost which parts of the garden seem to escape); or, if you can remember to do so, throw a piece of sacking round the root crown and it will respond by giving you more flowers in summer.

If you want a change from the traditional mauve and red flowers, look out for two varieties called "Margaret" and "Madame Cornelissen", both of which have red and white flowers. It pays, incidentally, to go to a specialist nursery for fuchsias if you're planning to buy several plants. Your local paper or a gardening magazine will give you addresses in your area.

Chrysanthemums are the kind of thing you either like or loathe, and that's that. My main objection to them is that while they do undoubtedly give you a wonderful display in the autumn, the plants look so darned bedraggled for the rest of the year. If you've inherited a batch and share my views on the subject, try doing something different with them: turn them into climbers instead. In the spring or in late autumn after they have flowered, move them so that they are against a wall or fence, then, when they start to grow again, choose the strongest shoot from each plant and peg it to the wall or tie it loosely to the trellis, nipping off all the other shoots. All the plant's energy will go into making that one shoot climb up the wall. You'll have fewer flowers, of course, but at least it will look different. (You can do the same thing, incidentally, with Michaelmas daisies and with geraniums.)

Laurel and *Privet* are the bane of the Victorian garden, the foundation of a respectable shrubbery, and a thorough nuisance, because they look so dank and depressing. There's little you can do to improve them, short of rooting them out, but if you haven't room or the inclination to plant something tall in front of them, try rooting a rampant climber near them and encourage it to smother them with something more attractive. Honeysuckle is good for this, so is the Russian vine, *Polygonum Baldshuanicum.*

Don't be afraid of moving your shrubs and small trees around if you fancy a change of scene. Most people are terrified of moving anything approaching the size of a bush, but if you are physically able to tackle it, and you treat the plant properly, it's a picnic. First of all, find out what kind of root system you're faced with. Some plants have roots which like the carrot grow obliging straight down into the earth, and they're the easiest to get out. Others have roots that are spread out like the fingers of your hand.

Loosen the soil all around the bush first, in a wide circle. Then rock the bush, gingerly, and notice where the earth surface moves – that's a sign that here's a root underneath. Then, using a fork (not a spade or you may chop straight through a vital artery of the plant), loosen the earth still more, and dig deeper than before. Rock the plant again, and see if it shows signs of coming out; carry on in this way until you are able to shift it. The essence of the whole thing is speed. Don't leave the roots exposed any longer than necessary. If the root system comes in a nice compact shape, then keep a goodish ball of soil around the plant when you move it so that the fuss is minimal. Never move plants on a frosty day, or when the ground is bone-dry – postpone operations until the soil is pleasantly moist and warm, it will be better for the plant, and easier for you, too.

Small trees can also be moved around. I've uprooted and transported by car some small apple trees from one garden to another three times now, without losing one. It sometimes sets them back for the first season afterwards, but it's still worthwhile. The secret of success with trees is to stamp the earth firmly down round them after you've replanted them. That's where a lot of people make mistakes – they don't tuck their plants and trees into bed firmly enough.

Something for nothing

One advantage of inheriting an old garden is that you can, with a little guile, spend virtually no money at all in keeping it well stocked up by doing a little propagation. Any fool can take cuttings, and it only takes a matter of minutes to do it; if you plant enough of them some are sure to grow. To give your cuttings the best chance, though, it pays to dig over a special bed for them in a corner, mixing in a little sand to lighten the soil. However, even if you don't do that you should have some successes. Cuttings need looking after until they have rooted properly, so if you're exposed to heavy winds and rain, if you have cats or dogs that are likely to knock the would-be plants for six, it's better to plop them into pots rather than into the ground.

Most hardwood plants, the flowering shrubs, evergreens, roses and fruit bushes, can be propagated in the autumn by this easy method. Choose a healthy-looking shoot of reasonable length, about a foot long (or less, if the plant is small), and pull it away from its parent branch, leaving if possible a little "heel" on the end of it. Pull off any lower leaves that might find themselves buried when you put the cutting in the ground and, if the shoot is very vigorous, nip off the top bud as well. Make a hole in the ground for the shoot and pop in a little sand, or firm it down in its specially prepared bed, then leave it until the following spring, by which time it should have rooted. That's all there is to it. Some cuttings will "take", and some won't, so always plant more than you'll need.

Some plants, rhododendrons and azaleas for instance, are propagated by layering. This is, if anything, even more simple. You just choose a likely-looking, low-growing branch and nick it with a sharp knife half-way along (don't cut as much as half-way through). You then bury this centre section, still attached to the parent plant, into the ground. I weight mine down with a stone on top to make sure that neighbourhood cats won't dig it up again. The nicked piece of the branch will, eventually, throw down its own roots, when you can turn it into a separate plant. Another way of layering is to bury the nicked section of stem into a largish flower-pot full of good soil. This is useful if the lower branches are not conveniently near to the ground.

Many herbaceous plants, like Michaelmas daisies for instance, are increased by division. Clumpy plants that have grown overlarge and are tending to sprawl can be divided into two by shoving two small hand forks or a fork and a trowel firmly into their middle, then pulling them apart, rather like the wishbone of a chicken. One half can then be shifted elsewhere. Strictly speaking, all herbaceous plants should be attended to in this way every three or four years.

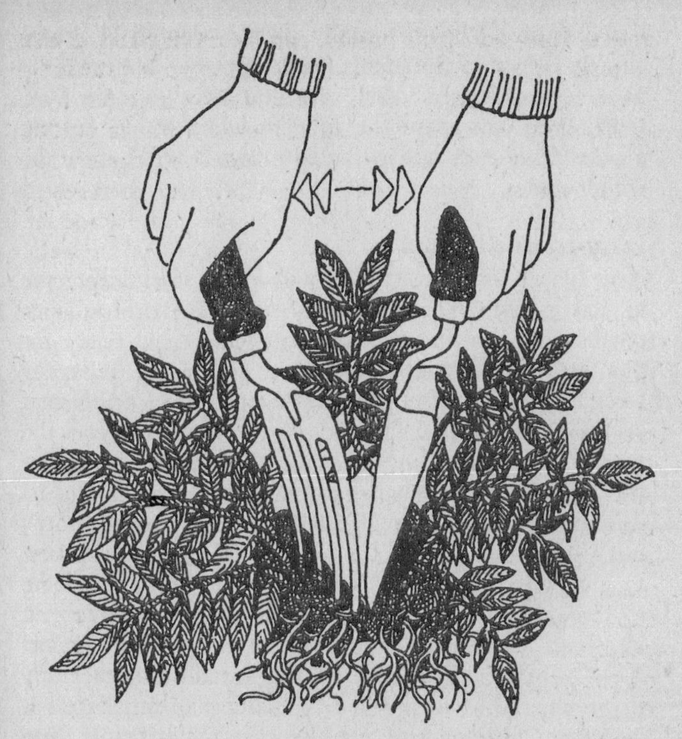

How to divide up an overgrown clump into smaller plants

I can't see any of us mincing round the garden, devotedly dead-heading our daisies, but there's no doubt that if you can be bothered to cut off dead flowers from time to time you'll be rewarded with fresh ones. The same goes for spiky things like lupins and delphiniums; if you chop off their flower spears once they're finished, you may get a second crop. The trouble with a herbaceous border is that it does tend to look untidy. You can cut down a lot of work by gradually substituting metal ring supports for the wooden stakes the previous owner had, no doubt, lovingly used. These supports are less obtrusive (they're usually plastic – coated in green) and they do stop the plants from leaning over drunkenly as they grow larger. You'll save that awful autumn look, too, if you can spare the time to whizz round cutting all the deadheads and withered brown leaves before the winter comes.

How-to-do-it notes

New plants for your garden will almost certainly come to you in pots. You've no doubt seen the professionals on the telly showing you how to decant them ready for planting, but in case you haven't, here goes: Put your forefinger and your middle finger either side of the stem of the plant at the base, to support it; now turn the plant pot upside-down and give it a smart tap on the side of a windowsill or whatever, and the plant and its surrounding soil should slide out happily. I say "should", but I've found that in the case of plastic pots it's best to give them a squeeze or two before they are willing to disgorge their contents. If your plants come to you in a box, carefully bang each of the sides in turn against a wall, then lay one edge on the ground and *carefully* tip it up, rather as if you were sliding an omelette out of a pan. Or you can use the cake-tin principle, and loosen the edges of the soil with a knife – the plants will then, we hope, spill gently out.

New paths in an old garden are no longer a problem. You can cheat now by using cold bitumen (sold under the name of Expandite), which will give you a tough garden path in no time at all. It's marvellous too for re-surfacing an existing path that has got rather tatty-looking. But it must be laid on a firm base. You can either use rubble with a layer of sand on top, or put it on top of existing concrete, which will need sealing first with a special solution. You can buy the asphalt/bitumen in half-hundredweight or hundredweight bags, together with the sealing compound, and you'll need half a hundredweight to the square yard. Bitumen paths need some sort of edge to them to stop them "fraying". A strip of wooden battening laid on edge will do, or a line of bricks, or you could use a lawn edging strip.

Another material worth looking into, for tarting up old paths, is something that you lay very much like roofing felt, but which gives a pleasant appearance and grip to materials like concrete. It's called Temple Pavex, and you should be able to find it in the larger gardening centres or at some hardware merchants.

4
WHO NEEDS GRASS?
LAWNS AND ALTERNATIVES

Just who will mow the lawn *this* time has been the near-cause of divorce in the nicest families. To many people it is the one gardening chore that they hate most of all, the start of the Sunday sulks.

He sits there, reading the paper while she hangs around, glowering, suggesting isn't it about time the grass was cut? Or worse still, she goes out and does it – and comes back indoors hating him.

Mowing the lawn is like cleaning the car. Some people love doing it, caressing the sides of their Ford with a polishing mop. But to other people it is something that is only done when the vehicle looks so disgusting that neighbourhood children have taken to writing messages on its dirty sides.

There are people who actually get a kind of hypnotic pleasure out of to-ing and fro-ing over their particular patch of grass. Others enjoy sublimating their power complex behind the handles of a motor mower – then there are the clippings to be carted away, the edges to be trimmed. Seriously though, having large areas of grass to take care of is not the problem it used to be, so grass might suit in your case. After all, power mowers take the back-breaking work out of it and you can keep down the daisies if they bother you by spraying them away. But there is only one way to keep grass in trim, and that is to cut it, often.

We learned that the hard way: we were once appointed gardeners to the Royal Navy. It sounds an unlikely story, but it's perfectly true. The only way we could stay aboard our boat on the island where we lived was to be employed by the Admiralty, who owned it.

So gardeners we became – fast. But trouble loomed ahead, quite apart from flowers knocked down and trampled on by Sea Cadets' boots on night exercises, for the Commander's wife was fond of gardening, and wanted the grass to be kept very short at all times.

As reluctant gardeners with only a hand mower (the Admiralty didn't run to motorised aids) we found the grass-cutting rather a pill. So we brilliantly – as we thought – invested in a pair of geese to do the job. Did they eat the grass? Yes, after a fashion, but then only when they fancied it, which was not very often. We'd reckoned without the fact that geese can swim – who'd have thought it?

More than once a week the boatyard down at Kingston Bridge would ring up and say, "Your geese are down here again, fighting with the swans". This was a particularly heinous crime since the swans belonged to the Queen, and the boatyard belonged to a Swan-Upper. We spent more time rowing up and down the Thames, goose-catching, than we would ever have done in mowing the lawn.

Some friends I know kept a goat as a grass-cutter. It not only cut the grass, it savaged it. It also stripped all their trees of every inch of bark and ate the clothes off the washing line. It butted the lady next door and attempted to rape a man who came to read the gas meter. They decided it was cheaper to switch to concrete.

Starting a lawn

If you settle for grass and you're beginning with a new lawn, don't be tempted to save money and sow grass-seed. By the time the ground has been prepared properly

– and you have to practically go down on your hands and knees and smooth it over with a tooth brush – you will be a nervous wreck. Then comes the fun of stringing cotton across it to discourage the birds (though in fairness, you can now buy seed ready-impregnated with anti-bird potion) and stopping the children/dog – worse still, other people's children/dogs – from dancing on it.

By the time the first tiny green shoots come through its bald surface, you are on tranquillisers, and rush out to see if the blades are weeds.

However, if you insist on sowing your own lawn, here goes: Beg, borrow or steal a special seed-hopper. Make sure the ground is as level as possible; some people I know even use a spirit level for the job, but unless you're planning a bowling green I wouldn't bother. The seed-hopper scatters its contents for you while you push it up and down like a lawn mower. (The biblical way of sowing seed is tiring on the arm and tends to give you lush green patches in one place, thin spots in another, but a seed-hopper guarantees more evenness.)

After the sowing is finished you rake the ground gingerly in a direction at right angles to the one you chose when you prepared the ground – if you'd raked it before from north to south, for instance, this time you do it from east to west. All that is left to do now is to sit back and wait about a month for the grass to appear. You'll be relieved to hear that it won't need cutting for a long time, until it is about 2½ inches high in fact.

How much seed will you need? You'll find instructions for calculating this on the packet. It's rather like ordering wallpaper – all you need to know is the square footage you plan to cover. But you can reckon roughly that you'll need 12 oz of seed to the square yard to allow enough for the inevitable moment when the packet falls over or the bag bursts and you lose some of it.

Turfing is much easier because it's so *instant* – one

minute you have a bare brown patch, the next you have a real lawn – but it's more expensive, too. Turves are usually 3 ft by 1 ft and are delivered (that usually means dumped on the pavement outside your house) rolled up like Swiss rolls.

If you're going to turf your garden you need *friends* to help you cart the stuff round the back and stack it ready for unrolling. You'll also need them to help you clear the boulders off the ground – which, we hope, you've already sprayed in good time with selective weed-killer.

Turves are laid brick-wall fashion, that is the joins between one row should come in the middle of the turves on the previous one. This usually means that you have to cut the turf at either end to fit. Don't disobey this instruction in the hope of saving a little cash – you may well end up with curious wavy lines in your lawn. (See illustrations overleaf.)

You can plonk down turf at any time of year, unless the climate has gone mad. But it's obviously bad planning to put them down in the middle of a summer drought, when you'll be out there dementedly watering the grass to keep it alive. Nor is it a very bright idea to try in midwinter when the ground is like iron. But within reason you can lay it throughout the year. If you do hit a patch of bad weather, leave the turves in a heap and water them – not too much, just enough to keep them fairly moist.

When the time comes to lay them, unroll them gingerly, for they tend to break, rather like my own home-made Swiss rolls. Once a turf is in place, give it a good whack with the back of a spade to bed it down, and push them all up as close together as you possibly can, rather like when laying tiles. Within about a month, if the weather has been reasonable, the turves should have grown together nicely and the joins have disappeared.

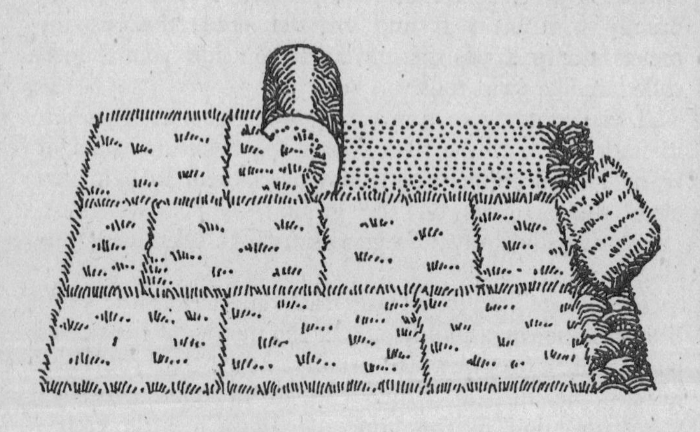

Making a new lawn with turves

Once you've laid your lawn it should need no more attention than occasional cutting and, if you're feeling kindly towards it, a spray or two with selective weed killer and liquid fertiliser mixed. Never mow the grass in winter when it is wet – as if you would! – the blades will drag some of the grass out of its moorings, squash the rest flat.

Don't make clear-cut edges to your lawn, no matter what anyone tells you. Above all don't bang in bits of plastic or tin to keep the edges straight. The lawn may look neater that way, it's true, but you'll either have to live with a row of whiskers along the side or spend hours on it with a pair of shears and an edging tool, and none of us are going to do *that*. Leave your lawn so that the mower glides happily over the edge of the grass.

If not a lawn

Supposing your garden is fairly small and you don't need a lawn, then why have one? There are plenty of alternatives. You could, for instance, have a pond. One woman I know has turned almost the whole of her pocket-sized garden into a pool. She had good access from the road, so she was able to get a contractor to dig a hole for her in half a day. Her main expenditure was on a free-form fibreglass pool in blue. She plonked it in, shovelled earth back around its side to support it, then covered its fibreglass lip with pieces of broken paving (there are now pool-side plants growing up between the cracks). And she has now planted around it one or two miniature trees which are reflected prettily in the water. Pools are no bother to keep in a pristine condition if you stock them with the right plants; any aquatic specialist will help you here. And if the water looks uninteresting just as it is, you can always grow water-lilies.

Another lazy way of building a pool without all the

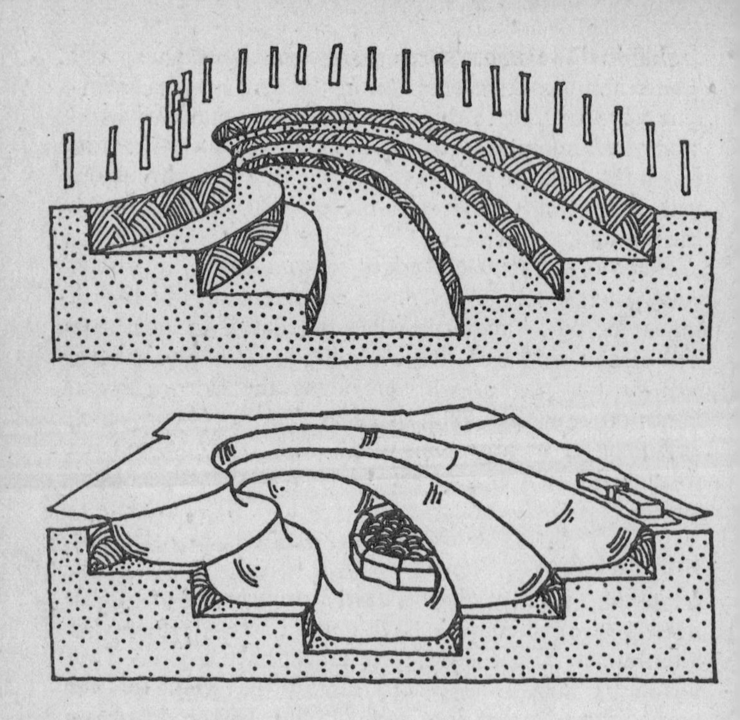

Cross-section diagrams showing two stages of making a lined pool – digging a shelved hole, and lining with heavy plastic sheeting

bother of using concrete is to use a flexible plastic liner, which looks like a giant ground-sheet. It's relatively easy to fix in place, and you don't necessarily have to dig out a pool shape to the full depth – it's possible to raise the sides a little with the excavated earth and cut down on the digging chore.

Here's how to make a lined pool: Stake out the rough outline you have in mind, avoiding as much as possible any right-angles – make it curvy rather than rectangular. Dig down a trench just one spade-depth inside this outline, then dig another shelf two spade-depths deep inside it. Continue in this fashion, making shelves, until you reach the centre. By doing this you have cheated – you have not had to dig out the whole pool to full depth and you have achieved stepped walls that are very unlikely to collapse on you, even when a heavyweight stands right on the edge. You can also, if you are feeling energetic, use these shelves to plant aquatic plants (you weight them down with stones).

Now you're ready to use your liner, but what size do you need? Calculating it is surprisingly easy – measure the length and the width of your pool at their fullest points, then add at least twice the maximum depth of the hole to each figure you come up with. Here's how: say your pool turns out to be 5 feet long, 3 feet wide and 2 feet deep (the minimum depth you can get away with, incidentally, is about 15 inches). Then the size of your liner should be 9 feet by 7 feet (i.e., 5+2+2 feet by 3+2+2 feet). Pool liners can be bought at garden centres or nursery shops. Never be tempted to buy just any old sheet of plastic – it needs to be specially reinforced.

Unroll the liner carefully over the pool, pat it down so that it clings to the shape, then anchor it with a few bricks or non-sharp stones at the bottom and along the shelves. You'll find it easier to do this operation, incidentally, on a summer day, when the plastic is slightly warm and more malleable.

Now shovel in an inch of soil or so on the floor of the pool and start to fill it with a hose. Don't do what I did and point it directly on the bottom, or you'll get splashed to high heaven. Direct the jet on the side of the pool instead.

Once the bottom is covered it's time to plant waterlilies or any other aquatic plants that you fancy.

There should now be at least 9 inches of plastic liner protruding over the edge of the pool like a frill. What to do with it? Cover it with stones, slabs or brick paving to keep it in place, hide it and make a decorative edge.

Chequerboard garden

Supposing you don't want a pool, or you've plenty of garden left over, what else can you do, instead of putting down grass? If the garden is small enough you can carve it up into squares like a giant chessboard and treat each one separately. (This dodge is particularly attractive in small backyards in town.) Take the size of your squares from the largest scale flagstones you can find, and lay them on a bed of sand at strategic points, using as many as you can afford; now decide what to do with the intervening squares – you could plant a small tree in one, fill the others with camomile or thyme – more about those useful carpeters in a minute – you can even fill a square attractively with old wine-bottle bottoms rammed safely broken-side down into a thin layer of cement, or pebbles treated the same way. Another square could be filled with miniature rock roses, dwarf crocuses, anything that is colourful and stays small.

Lawn but not grass

What can you do if you don't want grass as such but you like the look that it gives to a garden? If, for instance you scarcely use your garden at all, but you do want a pretty view from the window?

This is where two useful Alpines come in and lend a hand. They're two carpeting plants that no lazy gardener can afford to be without: camomile and raoulia. (I'm going to deal more fully with carpeting on ground cover plants in chapter 9.)

Raoulia is more like a mat than a plant to look at. Its leaves cling so close to the ground that it's impossible to believe that they are real. Held in the hand, a raoulia plant is rather like massed miniature mustard and cress. It looks like something for a doll's house garden, or those

Chequerboard effect for small garden

unbelievable Japanese indoor fireworks made from paper, which unfurl into tiny fronds when you set a match to them.

But raoulia gives, in general, the look of grass. It does have flowers in fact, but these are so small that you hardly notice them. There are several different varieties of raoulia to choose from, of course, but the kind that makes the most marvellous grass substitute is *Raoulia tenuicaulis*, which spreads nice and quickly, doesn't mind in the least being trodden on, and gives you a carpet of unbelievable bright emerald, rather like the film of green you get over a millpond. In fact it does rather make a lawn that looks like a stagnant pool, so much so that you're nervous of treading on it at first.

To make a lawn of raoulia you need to allow roughly one plant for every square foot to be on the safe side, every 2 square feet if you don't mind having bald patches on show while you wait. It'll take time anyway for the plants to join up, just as it does for grass to really make a lawn.

Raoulia is at its happiest in its own home surroundings, on a light, well-drained, slightly rocky soil. If your garden is inclined to be soggy, then you'll have to give this plant a miss. A really heavy clay soil simply doesn't give it the right kind of conditions – the wet earth tends to cling to its tiny leaves and smother them. If your ground is fairly normal, however, you can kid raoulia along quite happily into thinking it has Alpine conditions to live in, until it's properly established, when it won't care a jot, and will simply romp away throttling everything else in its path. A confidence trick on raoulia is quite simple: you just sprinkle coarse sand or gravel around the baby plants as you put them in, and leave it at that. Once they are thriving you can forget about them and they never need cutting.

Give the plant a fighting chance though; before you put it in, make sure that the ground is free from weeds, using a short-term weedkiller beforehand, in good time for planting. Raoulia won't let any weeds through once it has gained a good hold on the ground.

If you want something different, you can always have a multi-coloured lawn by using some of the other raoulias. *Raoulia australis*, for instance, makes a silvery coloured carpet that is very attractive, particularly in sunlight. It has tiny flowers of pale yellow, but it doesn't spread quite as vigorously as *Raoulia tenuicaulis,* so you'll need almost twice as many plants to cover the same area. *Raoulia glabra* is a little larger than the other two – it is darker green in colour and has tiny, starry, whitish flowers. But it spreads even less than the other two – it will cover an area about 8 inches square with luck.

Camomile is another carpeter that makes a good substitute for grass. There's a camomile lawn, incidentally, at Buckingham Palace, so if it is good enough for the Queen it should be good enough for you too.

Camomile's real name is *Anthemis nobilis*, and it used to be made into herbal tea. The Spaniards call it 'little apple" and use it to flavour one of their wines, Manzilla. The French use it for infusions for the liver. But we seem for some reason or other to neglect it. Drake is supposed to have played his famous game of bowls on a camomile lawn, but strangely enough you rarely if ever see bowling greens made from it these days.

The ordinary camomile, which looks very much like grass but is in fact coarser in texture and darker in colour than the average lawn, does need cutting from time to time, but not as frequently as grass does, and it has one advantage over the latter: it gives off a delicious scent when you crush it or tread on it.

In the summer the camomile flowers look like tiny white daisies. The great advantage of camomile is that it doesn't mind a drought. When an ordinary lawn is looking very sorry for itself indeed, and the sprinklers are out, camomile still seems green and happy. In fact it must have a lightish, porous soil, since, like raoulia, it hates to have a sticky clay-like bed to lie in.

The ordinary version of camomile is not the best one to choose for a lawn, neither is the double version, *Anthemis nobilis fl. pl.,* though the latter does only need cutting once, early in the season. For a lawn of any size, rather than a patch of green, *Anthemis nobilis* "Treneague" is the camomile to use. It doesn't flower, for one thing, and it never ever needs to be cut. It can be used too for carpeting the ground under shrubs (though it doesn't like trees), for it will choke any weeds on sight. Although it only grows a couple of inches high, it still has that delightful fragrance. The other types of camomile can be cut by mower if necessary, but don't have the blade set too low or the plants may be dragged out of the ground.

If you want to go all medieval and make your own camomile tea, it is quite simple – you can even get the ingredients from a herbalist. Pick 5–6 camomile flowers when they are in full bloom and dry them off in the sun or in a warm room until they almost crumble under your fingers. Put them in a jug, pour ½ pint of boiling water over them; when the infusion has stood for about 10 minutes, strain off the liquid and sweeten it with sugar.

There are two other plants which can be used to make lawns, but they are not, strictly speaking, like grass to look at. *Cotula squalida* spreads out to a firm carpet in a shade of olive green, with feathery leaves, but in autumn the leaves have a tendency to turn brownish, which gives a rather parched look. Thyme spreads happily to make a lawn, but your lawn in this case will be silver-pink or purple, not green. However it will quite happily stand up to being trodden on. *Lippea repens* is another carpeting plant which is inclined to be rather straggly, but its pretty pink flowers enliven it all through mid-summer and it spreads quickly. This, too, doesn't mind being walked over.

5
REMEMBER THAT OTHER DIMENSION

COVERING UP WITH CLIMBERS AND HEDGES

When you're working out what to do with the garden, don't forget that other vital dimension – UP. For there's a lot you can do to give the illusion of a well-kept profusion of plants, and a lot you can hide, too, by the clever use of hedges, climbers and screening.

If you've been handed out chain link for your garden fence, you may want to hide it with something, fast. It's a pity that we're so conventional and uninspired in our choice of hedges – few people ever dream of mixing several different shrubs together, for instance, to give a bit of variety (an idea that's particularly good in a long, thin garden); even a mixture of several different kinds of shrubs from the same species will liven things up a little.

Hedge shrubs

People *will* try to sell you privet. It has one advantage – it's cheap. But keep right away from it, whatever you do. Not only does it look nasty, except possibly in its golden form, but it needs trimming several times a year, and whoever wants to do that?

What you choose depends, of course, on what you want a hedge *for*. If it is to keep out neighbourhood dogs and children, you can't really beat the good old hawthorn; after all, farmers have used it for this purpose for years. It grows into a really tough thicket that nothing can penetrate, once it has got going.

Hawthorn is usually sold under its official Latin name of *Crataegus*. Don't just pick the ordinary common thorn, though, but go one better: choose *Crataegus oxyacantha*, the double crimson thorn, which has a positive profusion of deep pinky-red flowers, or *Crataegus arnoldiana*, which bears very large fruit in the autumn. The Glastonbury thorn, *C. monogyna* "Biflora", flowers twice in a year – in late spring and again in mid-winter, as a bonus, just when everything in the garden is looking dead. *Crataegus azarolus* is a particularly unusual form of the thorn, with larger, white flowers than the rest which come in large clusters, streaked with purple, and in the autumn it bears orange fruit which you can eat, if you want to – at the least, you know the children won't be poisoned if they take a fancy to them.

Thorn hedges don't need pruning or cutting, that's another of their great advantages, but you can snick back the dead wood if you want to, and although they shed their leaves in winter, the twigs that they leave form a dense fence. I think hawthorns look better in suburban or country surroundings than right in town, where they can seem sadly out of place.

If you're prepared to sit and wait a little, holly makes an ideal hedge. Not only is it evergreen, but it's also just as dense as the hawthorn and gives you the added bonus of your own Christmas decoration on the spot. Holly can grow 12 feet high and it doesn't in the least mind the smog and smoke of a town, or even the salty winds of the seaside. If it's berries you're after, though, be sure to buy a female holly plant to ensure a good supply.

Ilex aquifolium is the correct name for the common English holly which is used for Christmas decorations. If you want something a little more out of the ordinary, buy *Ilex aquifolium* "Argenteo-marginata Pendula", the silver weeping holly which produces great clusters of berries, too. For yellow berries instead of red, ask for "Bacciflava" – a hedge with alternate red- and yellow-berried hollies would make an unusual sight.

Chinese holly (*Ilex ciliospinosa*) has non-prickly leaves and the berries come egg-shaped instead of round, while Japanese holly (*Ilex crenata*) is a slow grower, but produces unusual berries that are purply-black in colour. For a really spiky hedge try *I. aquifolium* "Ferox", which has abnormally prickly leaves and won't let anything through. You can get it silver or gold-flecked, too.

The copper beech makes a cheap, quick-growing hedge that naturally looks very attractive both in spring, when the leaves unfurl in a pretty pale green, and in the autumn, when they turn that well-known red-gold colour. Beech leaves tend to stay put through most of the winter, even though it is of course a deciduous tree, but they have a habit of shedding in early spring and making a mess all over the grass. Providing, then, that you're planting other shrubs in front to disguise the fact that there are leaves all over the place, beech is a good choice for cheapness' sake. *Fagus sylvatica* is the correct name for the most common variety; *Fagus sylvatica* "Cuprea" is the real deep-toned copper beech, and there's a more purply variety, too – *F. sylvatica* "Purpurea".

A chain-link fence will make a first-class host to a hedge of rambling roses. An old rose called *Rosa* "Gloire des Rosomanes", recently given a lot of publicity under the name "Trail-blazer", is claimed to grow particularly fast – a growth of 18 inches a year – but I haven't tried it myself. You buy it in little bushes, plant them 10 inches apart, then sit back and wait result. Rose hedges are also good to disguise those rather awful post-and-

Free-growing rose hedge to hide an uninteresting fence

wire fences you get on some new housing estates. The flowering currant – try "King Edward VII" – also makes a good quick hedge.

If you've inherited a hedge, but don't particularly like what you've been given, you can smother it quite successfully in summer with rambling roses. "Albertine" blooms early and gives you clusters of delicate salmon pink flowers; you could mix it with "Purity", which flowers later and has white blooms.

Almost any climber can be persuaded to wander over a hedge and liven it up a little, and clematis and honeysuckle are both particularly obliging in this way.

The firethorn (*Pyracantha*) is almost always strung up against the wall of a house as if it were a climber, but left to itself it will make a first-class hedge for you, and give you double value for your money: first of all clusters of tiny white flowers in the spring, and then in the autumn a fantastic array of bright red berries. Don't grow it too near concrete paths or patios – the berries will drop, or be taken off by the birds, and will splatter all over the place, making an appalling mess. *Pyracantha coccinea* "Lalandii" is a good variety to choose. Once it is well grown, you will have a glorious show of red berries when autumn comes, almost as if the bush were on fire.

For screens and trellises

Dustbins and other dreadful items of domestic impedimenta need screening from our sight wherever they are. Screens are useful, too, for shutting off part of the garden from the rest – perhaps the end where there's a rubbish heap or a shed for tools and bicycles – but they need to be put up really securely if they're not going to develop into a nightmare. Too many people have light-heartedly erected a trellis, then grown ivy (one of the most lethal climbers of all time) all over it, and wondered why it came crashing down. All fencing and screening, even if it is an artful arrangement of whitewashed wooden boughs made into a loggia, needs to have supporting posts that are dug down deep and concreted in – otherwise it's wiser to grow a hedge. Anyone who has had fence trouble, seeing the side wall of the garden first lean in, then start to clatter to the ground, knows what havoc is wreaked by the timber when it comes down, so don't stint in this respect; hire an expert if you can, to put the posts in for you – you'll find it relatively easy to do the rest.

Trellis need not have quite such strong support if it is artfully arranged, and the same goes for lightweight interwoven wood. Erect it in panels at right-angles to each other, like three sides of a square, round the dustbins, and it will support itself with a minimum of below-

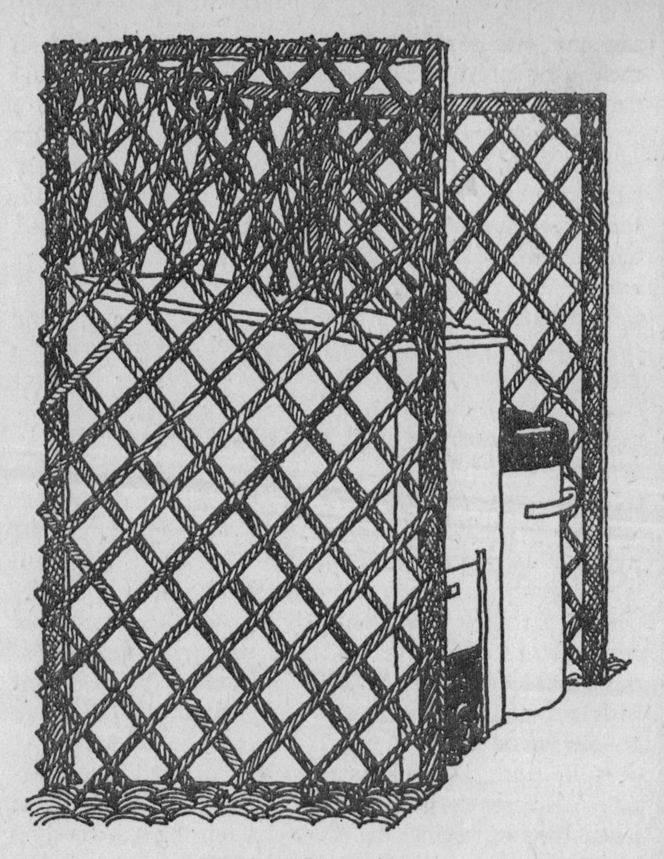

Trellis to hide dustbins, etc.

the-ground support, or zig-zag it like a half-open screen – that's another way to cheat. The fence that is most likely to fall over is the one that presents a large flat area to the prevailing wind, so be cunning and avoid asking for trouble in this way.

There are some particularly useful plants that will act as a temporary screen until you've got around to putting up that wall or piece of fencing, and they can remain there afterwards to help decorate it. They're flowering perennials that grow to a particularly useful height.

The plume poppy (*Macleaya*) will grow up to 8 feet tall for you; it puts out huge leaves, like outstretched hands, that are silver-green on top, silver-pink beneath, then tall sprays of flowers in mid-summer. It is good and strong and needs no staking, unless you put it somewhere where the wind whistles through, and it will form a front for a slow-growing hedge, or hide a row of dustbins or a coal-bunker quite happily. In time you can turn it into a kind of hedge by dividing the clumps into two and increasing their number.

Our old friend the sunflower (*Helianthus*) makes a marvellous screen and will stand almost any type of soil, so long as it has some sun to cheer it up. The tallest sunflower of the lot is "Monarch", which will shoot up as much as 7 feet, with "Loddon Gold", which gets to about 6 feet, as a runner-up. *Helianthus decapetalus* "Maximus" is the variety to choose if you want really large flowers. Like the plume poppy, the sunflower is simply increased by dividing the plant. (Make sure, incidentally that you get the perennial sunflower, not the annual version.)

A third good, quick, screening plant is the rudbeckia, which, like the sunflower, can be bought either as an annual or a perennial. It has an impressive shower of daisy-like flowers, usually with dark brown velvety centres and yellow leaves. "Golden Glow" grows the tallest, shooting up to around 7 feet, with "Herbstsonne", which gets up to about the same height, and has green centres to its flowers. Another variety, "Golden Ball", has double daisies, but it only reaches 6 feet tall.

Two great little helpers that anyone who has screening problems should know about are solanum and garrya, shrubs which are climbers as well. So you can start them off as bushes on the site if you want to, to hide

Living screen of sunflowers

things temporarily, then train them up over the trellis or fence you erect later on.

Solanum crispum, the Chilean potato tree, is a semi-evergreen shrub which thrives in a fairly sheltered, sunny spot, like a wall facing south, for instance. It's a fast mover once it's planted, and it can easily reach 15 feet in height, if left unchecked. Buy the variety *Solanum crispum* "Autumnale" for choice, because its prolific rash of purple-mauve flowers lasts well into the autumn.

Garrya eliptica is another shrub that turns into a rampant climber if you let it. And it might well have been designed for the lazy gardener, because it never needs any pruning. Plant it against a sheltering wall, or where one is going to be, and it will shoot up to about 12 feet high and spread 8 feet wide in the space of a couple of years – how's that for coverage! It comes from America, where they call it the silver tassel plant. Its flowers are nothing much to shout about, but it is prized mainly for its giant catkins of a splendid silvery-green, which hang down in great profusion like tassels of silk. Sex rears its ugly head when you're buying this shrub – be sure to ask for a male plant if you want catkins; the female plants bear thick clusters of black fruit instead. *Garrya elliptica* is worth considering any time on its own merits as a bush, not just as a climber.

Commonsense about climbers

Don't grow climbers up against the side of your house unless there's a reason – why give everyone else a free show that you can't see yourself? Our house, which is an old one, has the most fantastic climbing roses which go up to the third storey, but we never get a glimpse of them unless we lean out of the window, and they face a part of the back garden where we never sit. They tend to blow down in gales and are a hellish nuisance to fix, and if they get blight, mildew or any of the other things to which roses are prone, we need a fireman's ladder to reach them, even with a spray. Climbers are tremendously useful aids, however, if you want to graft a new piece of house on to an old building – a rapid-growing creeper grown over the new bald concrete building will make it blend in better. But remember, if you're putting up any sort of wall that you know you want to grow climbers against, be smart and save yourself time and energy – get the builder to knock little metal "eyes" into the mortar between the bricks or into the concrete screening, so that you've got tie-up points ready and waiting.

If you don't have staging posts readymade in your wall, and you are not training your plant up something with accommodating holes in it, like trellis, be careful to pick climbers that can look after themselves and don't need tying up – like the pretty *Hydrangea petiolaris*, which will wander all over a wall quite happily and find its own places to cling to.

Another climbing member of the hydrangea family is *Decumaria barbara*, which has one up on the *petiolaris* in that it is semi-evergreen. It reaches up to 30 feet in height and has small white flowers, but it is more expensive to buy. Yet another distant cousin, *Pileostegia viburnoides*, is not very often grown, which is a pity because it looks so good. It has long, glossy, evergreen leaves and produces white flowers in the late summer and autumn, just when other plants are beginning to fade. All these climbers will cling to a wall, once they are established, without needing to be tied up.

Ivy is of course the most clingy climber of the lot. Once it has got a grip on the wall it is there for keeps. Its embrace is so loving, however, that it tends to tear out the mortar between your bricks and pull things over, so keep ivy where it should be, for ground cover – let it strangle the weeds instead. There are other self-clinging climbers that are not as vicious as ivy, but still look after themselves. Let's take a look at a few:

Metal 'eyes' inserted before you plant a climber will greatly simplify the job of training it up a wall

The poor old Virginia creeper is one of the most maltreated of all plants, grown as it so often is against the walls of the house, when it becomes commonplace and nasty.

In autumn, when its leaves turn colour, the Virginia creeper looks thoroughly hot and bothered against red brick, where it usually seems to grow. But train it up against a snow-white wall and it can look fabulous. A good place to grow it is on a party wall edging your plot – treat the wall first with white cement paint, and then grow the creeper over it. You wouldn't recognise it as your old suburban friend, it looks so chic.

The true Virginia creeper, *Parthenocissus quinquefolia,* is a really rampant grower and produces unbelievably bright green leaves in spring, which turn vivid orange and scarlet when autumn comes. But the best clinger of all is the smaller variety, *Parthenocissus tricuspidata* "Veitchii", which sticks to the wall like glue. If you want something more exotic there's always *Parthenocissus himalayana,* which has slightly larger leaves that turn a really deep crimson colour in autumn, and produces clusters of small deep blue "grapes". Another even more unusual member of the family is *Parthenocissus henryana,* which comes from China, and produces purple and white striped leaves in semi-shade, and red leaves in the autumn. The type of Virginia creeper to avoid, however, like the plague, is *Parthenocissus inserta,* because, unlike the rest of the family it uses tendrils for climbing and needs support. But it will very happily take over a tree or a bush and smother that without any staking or tying up.

For a really showy display among climbers that will do their own clinging, the schizophragma, an Asiatic plant, gives good value for money and will cling happily by itself to a brick wall. There are two species that you can buy in this country, the Chinese one, which has large cream-coloured flower clusters, and the Japanese version, which is smaller and has pale yellow flowers. The sunnier the spot in which they are planted, the more flowers they will give you. Another possibility to consider is the *Ercilla volubilis,* a completely evergreen climber from Chile which produces lots of spikes of small white flowers quite early in the spring.

In this life, as we all know, you can't have everything, and to get a really showy display of flowers in a climber you have to go for the varieties that need tying to the wall. But if you've organised things properly, and have nails or loops ready fixed, the job need not be too arduous. Save yourself trouble in the future, though – make the loops generously wide so there's no danger the plant will be strangled as the stems swell with age, and use plastic-covered wire, or something similarly indestructible – string and raffia tend to rot in time, and ordinary wire will rust.

Clematis and wistaria are the two most popular climbers around; like rose- and bulb-growers, nurserymen who specialise in clematis are very thick on the ground and do a lot to promote the plant. But be warned, once you go off the beaten track with clematis you're venturing into the territory of the impassioned gardener. Some of the newer hybrids need a lot of nursing, and even then will mysteriously wilt and die on you on occasions, without any rhyme or reason.

So it pays the lazier gardener to stick to the old faithfuls like *Clematis montana*, which produces a profusion of white or pink flowers (if you want pink, ask for *Montana rubens*) and which can be relied upon to behave itself. Of the large-flowered hybrid clematis which have been developed, *Clematis jackmanii* is the most reliable and the most showy plant to choose with its large violet-purple flowers. But if the cult of the clematis interests you, and you're willing to take a chance, you can choose hybrid plants in almost any colour you fancy, or, among the older smaller-flowered plants there are several evergreens to choose from, including *Clematis balearica,* the fern-leaved clematis, which comes from the Balearic Islands and has foliage that turns bronze-coloured in the winter. But I'm decidedly vulgar in my tastes, and would stick to *jackmanii* any time, or *jackmanii superba,* which is the toughest of the lot.

Clematis will take to almost any soil, but the plant likes its roots shaded, which is not difficult if you plonk a bushy evergreen next to it. Nobody knows what causes clematis to wilt suddenly, but it only seems to happen to the hybrids with their large luscious flowers, so it's a wise move to plant two close together, just in case one lets you down.

Wistaria is a rather more lady-like climber and its colourings are more delicate. When it is grown over a wall or like a vine across the roof of a conservatory, its long tassels of scented lavender flowers – some of them a foot in length – hang in waterfalls of colour.

Wistaria is more woody than clematis and can be trained in several versatile ways: pruning it back can make it into a bushy shrub, or you can turn it into a small weeping standard tree (it looks pretty by a pond this way) by allowing only one main shoot to grow at first, then encouraging it to spread. Its common name is the grape-flower vine, and it can be found with white flowers (*W. floribunda* "Alba") or in a double-flowered form (*W. floribunda* "Violaceo-Plena").

Wistaria is a very well-behaved climber, but it doesn't always know its own strength – I once saw one that had almost topped a rather spindly tree. However, if you train it up a sturdy old deciduous tree in the garden, it will cover it with a riot of colour during its long flowering season.

If you want something pretty to cover a fence or an archway quickly try the old-fashioned honeysuckle, an up-stage relative of the woodbine, with its splendid scent. Plant two different varieties together, and you can have a continuous display of flowers throughout the summer. The early and late Dutch – *Lonicera periclymenum* "Belgica" and "Serotina" – will do the job very splendidly for you, giving you flowers through from May to October. If it's speed that you're after, choose *Lonicera americana*, which is very strong and grows at a splendid rate.

Climbers are often used to hide an eyesore, an unattractive but essential shed, for instance, and since we don't want to see the monstrosity any more in winter than in summer, it's commonsense to choose an evergreen climber for the purpose. There are two varieties of Honeysuckle that come to the rescue in this way. *Lonicera alseuosmoides* obligingly keeps its leaves, all the year round and produces yellow and purple flowers in mid-summer, blue-black berries later on; *Lonicera henryi* has glossy, dark-green foliage and blue black berries, too, while its flowers are red and yellow in colouring. *Giraldi,* another Chinese evergreen honeysuckle, has smaller, purple-red flowers and is particularly good at twining itself into a dense mass.

Jasmine is usually thought of as a shrub, but it will climb quite happily to a height of up to 15 feet if allowed, and can be trained any way you wish. *Jasminum nudiflorum,* the famous winter jasmine which can always be relied upon to give a delicate starry mass of yellow in midwinter, does well on a wall facing north or east, when many other climbers would protest. There are one or two evergreen versions, but the only one worth risking in any sort of exposed spot is *J.diversifolium* "Glabricymosum", which comes from Asia, but which does not grow very high.

6
THROW AWAY THAT SPADE!
GET MECHANISED

A machine – any sort of machine, in fact – is the non-gardener's best friend, for several reasons...

It's more fun to use, for one thing, than employing one's own manual labour on any heavy task. Most of us nowadays would rather spend hours wrestling with a piece of machinery than actually getting down on our hands and knees and doing the work. We delude ourselves into thinking we're being labour-saving that way.

If you've got a machine, you can often persuade some other mug to take over the whole chore, simply by saying, "Have you tried my new mower/cutter/flame-thrower?" Then thrusting the thing into his hands and leaving him to it. Before he knows where he is, poor sap, everyone has fled indoors and he's doing the work. What's more, he has to pretend that he's enjoying it.

Machines don't lose their tempers and go home to mother or get tired, and they don't sulk, either. And provided you look after them reasonably well (like *not* leaving them out in the rain for days) they'll do a lot of the nastier gardening chores for you, and you can even persuade yourself that you enjoy using them.

When should you buy and when should you hire? It always pays to hire any machine at first, to make sure that you are happy with it; some of the more enlightened shops will lend one to you to try out. And although it may end up to their disadvantage if you find you don't like the thing at all, it's always a good idea to avail yourself of an offer like this.

Having used a machine on loan, and found it is just what you want, then comes the query, whether or not to buy.

It never pays to acquire any item of machinery for the garden unless you are going to use it frequently. Machines of any kind are at their happiest when they are being used, and anything that is going to be dumped in a corner of the garage and left there in the damp for half the year will be sheer hell to start when you want to take it out again. Meanwhile, it's yet another piece of household clutter to trip over.

A mower or a digger that is only used very occasionally, and then for only a short time, is a sheer nuisance to look after. If you're not careful, the time taken on getting it out, setting it up, then putting it away again, can outweigh its usefulness in doing the work for you, so if your lawn is really pocket-handkerchief-sized you're better off with a hand-mower and a willing Boy Scout instead. Remember, too, that machines depreciate at an alarming speed, and should you want to sell it again you'll be surprised to find that the very dealer who enthused over it when he sold it to you will sadly declare, that the model is now obsolete, if you try to sell it back to him.

The indispensable mower

Anyone who has decided to grass over most of the garden should certainly spend some money at once on a decent motor mower to cope with it (we'll come to the different types available in a moment). And if you're insisting on having neat hedges, then an electric clipper will snick off a great deal of time spent wobbling on top of a pair of steps with a pair of shears in your hand. Enquire around first, though – it may be that you have a neighbour who would buy one in partnership with you. Garden machinery is one of the rare things that two can share, happily. Come to think of it, if your hedge looks *that* wild, perhaps the neighbours would club together and buy you a hedge-clipper as a present! Hedge-clippers, too, are dealt with later in more detail.

A mower is the most useful, most used piece of garden equipment you can buy ready mechanised, but make sure first of all which kind is for you.

There are two basic types of grass-cutting machines, and the one that you want depends on the amount, and the type, of grass that you're stuck with.

The motor mower proper works with a cylindrical set of revolving blades and a roller behind, and is a motorised version of the old pull-and-push. It clings closely to the ground (though the "set" of the blades can be raised and lowered a little), and it cuts the grass skin-head length for that bowling green finish everyone hankers after. Having read that, you may already be thinking that this machine is perhaps not for you. It has in fact two main disadvantages: it cannot be used if the ground is wet, for it will skid all over the place, and it can't be used if you let the grass grow too high (are you beginning to get the message?). It also has another disadvantage: there's a natty little box at the back for grass cuttings, which is always too small for the job and which frequently needs emptying.

Motorised lawn-mowers start with the petrol-engined variety, the most popular makes around, but let me sound a word of warning here: don't go for the lightest, cheapest one you can find. Some of them are far too flimsy for us lazy gardeners – they're rather like pedigree dogs that need constant loving attention if they are not to fall ill. Many lightweight machines, if casually handled, will literally shake themselves to pieces before

Electric lawn-mower

your very eyes – and there's nothing more irritating, believe me, than spending a sunny Sunday afternoon on you hands and knees in the middle of the lawn, to the tune of ribald laughter, searching for some lost nut or bolt. So if you're buying the conventional motorised mower, get one that looks good and solid and not too tinny, make sure that it has a guarantee, and that there are servicing arrangements near at hand (some firms

Z

will collect and deliver for you). Don't get one that's too small, either. You'll have twice as much walking up and down to do, and many hideous journeys to and from the rubbish heap with that little box. If you've any serious amount of grass to tackle, you'll need a machine that is 14 inches wide at least, so don't be overcome by the dinkiness of the mini-mower.

Electric lawn-mowers are the lightest of the lot, and on the face of it have many advantages. You simply plug them in and get going – no string-pulling. But they frighten me stiff for two reasons: If you are unlucky enough to mow over your own cable you're more than likely to mow the lawn no more – it can give you a fatal shock. And if you've lots of fiddly pieces of lawn to do, and trees and bushes to mow around, you're going to get into a terrible tangle with the cable trailing here and there and, more likely than not, pulling out of its socket as it's strained to breaking point. Mowing a cluttered garden with an electric mower is like trying to vacuum-clean in a room full of furniture – be warned.

You can get around the safety bit by buying a battery-operated mower. But the very weight of the battery itself, which you have to hump around with you of course, takes away some of the advantage of an electrically powered machine. Then you have to keep re-charging the thing, which is a nuisance. There always seems to be the awful moment, as all the lawn is done except the middle, when the battery runs out, the machine grinds to a halt and you have to wait for hours before you can use it again.

Batteries need replacing from time to time, too, which is costly. And if you're the kind of person who always forgets to check that the battery in your car is topped up with distilled water . . . forget it, the battery mower is not for you!

What about the third type, rotary cutters? A rotary

Rotary cutter

cutter will also keep the grass short. It may not give you quite that bowling-green finish, but it's practical, reliable and for indolent gardeners like us, the answer to our prayers.

This machine, which is more squared-off in shape than the motor mower, has a windmill of 4 blades, or fewer, under a metal cover; these whirl round, propeller fashion, parallel to the lawn, and mince up the grass nice and finely.

The great advantage of the rotary cutter over the other kinds of machines is that it will tackle virtually any kind of grass, from those nasty, slippery spikes of couch grass that skid out from under an ordinary mower and stick up stiffly like bristles afterwards, to the rough, tough grass that grows by the sea. It will tackle grass of almost any height, unlike the motor mower, which baulks at anything above an inch or so, and you can use it in bad weather – while the neighbours are indoors gnashing their teeth, you can waltz out over the lawn and cut it without any fear of damaging the grass.

But, if you're after that fine, velvety finish, forget about the rotary cutter. Your garden will look rather more like a well-kept playing field than a specimen lawn at Kew, and you won't have those nice stripes that an ordinary mower gives you, either. However, think of all the advantages: you don't have to pick up the grass – the cuttings are so fine that they can be left scattered on the lawn (unless the grass was extra long), and you can neglect the lawn for a while if you don't feel like tackling it, without the fear that you'll have to take a scythe to it afterwards. If you're likely to have a lot of *long* grass to cut, it pays to buy a box for the rotary cutter, otherwise your garden may look a little like Farmer Jones' hayfield when the grass cuttings dry off. (If you need a rake anyway, try to get hold of a traditional wooden farm one, rather than the metal variety. For one thing, the wooden one is more attractive to look at and better balanced to handle; for another it rakes up the grass cuttings without scoring the lawn like a vegetarian vampire.)

A small rotary cutter is perfectly easy to push around, provided it hasn't got puny little wheels that will tend to stick in dips and on bumps. If you have a really large area of grass to cope with, you could splurge out and buy a larger self-propelled model, but make sure that you can handle it – some types which will cope with brambles and undergrowth, too, are positively elephantine in their size and weight. Make sure that you can start it – it sounds silly, I know, but a lot of people buy machines without having ever once tried to get them going, and sometimes the very business of starting them up becomes an unpleasant shock to their system. Choose a model with a self-winding starter; the laborious business of putting all that string back to restart the engine is a tiresome nuisance, as anyone who has had dealings with an outboard engine on a boat will testify.

If you want to be really different in your dealings with the the lawn, there's now a grass cutter which works on the hovercraft principle and floats just above the surface of the ground. It starts in the usual way, puffs itself up and moves around on its own air cushion, and it's particularly good if the ground is uneven, for it just floats over the top with gay abandon; it's good for edges, too. But it is uncanny to handle at first, until you get used to it.

For Hedge-fanciers

If you're landed with a hedge that you have to trim for some reason – possible because half of it belongs to your next-door neighbour – it may pay you to buy your own electric hedge-cutter. The ordinary plug-in variety is reasonably safe if you make a habit of keeping the cable slung over your shoulder behind you at all times, but the very fact that it has a cable attached to it can be a nuisance. If you're worried about the possibility of a shock, you can buy a kind that works on a low voltage with the aid of a transformer, but that is rather a nuisance to organise.

The safest and least noisy clipper of the lot is the

Electric hedge-cutter

one that works without a cord at all, as it has a battery in the handle, but it can be rather heavy to hold up in the air for any length of time. There's another one that works off a car battery, and yet another that can be worked off your cultivator, if you have the right kind of machine (see below).

The gen about cultivators and flame guns

It's not really likely that you'll want to *buy* yourself a cultivator – unless you've had a change of heart over the garden by now – but here, for reference when hiring, is a quick run-down of the different types that you can get:

There are two main categories, those which are power-driven and walk by themselves, and the types which have the engine driving directly to the digging part – it revolves, and you push the machine along. The smaller cultivators come into this category, but they're not as bad as they sound, for the movement of the ploughing piece does help to drag the machine forward.

The larger, heavier type of cultivator is not really for you, unless you have an estate to look after. For one thing, all cultivators are surprisingly unwieldy to handle; turning them round corners is like trying to drive a double-decker bus round a bend, and dodging trees and shrubs with them is more difficult than you'd think. So it's best to get the smallest, sturdiest type you can find, unless you are doing a preliminary all-over dig on a bald new garden.

A cultivator doesn't dig up the soil in the way that you would with a spade, so don't expect the same results. Instead, it nibbles at the ground rapidly, leaving it ploughed in rough furrows and broken up into small pieces, so if you're going to plant anything delicate, the soil will, alas, need raking over first.

If the ground is well covered with weeds, it pays to spray it with the appropriate weed-killer *before* you use the cultivator, otherwise you're simply burying a lot of trouble for yourself later on. If the machine sticks when you're using it, make sure first that it isn't up against a stone or sitting on a lump of hard earth. It never pays to try to force the cultivator – or any other motorised machine, for that matter – over an obstruction, for almost inevitably the engine stalls and you have to start it all over again.

Cultivators offer all sorts of permutations, and if you have some digging and some mowing to do, it might pay you to get a machine that also has a rotary grass-cutting attachment, instead of buying a grass-cutter as a separate item. There's even a machine that will play host to all sorts of attachments, including artful aids like a hedge-cutter, and you can saw logs, too, with its help.

Many men, especially ex-army officers, for some reason I've never been able to figure out, are attracted to the idea of mowing down weeds with a flame gun. If the ground is dry, the weeds isolated and unsoggy, it works quite well, especially for lightweight weeds without deep roots. It has the advantage that you can re-plant the ground right away if you want to, with no bother about toxins left over from insecticides and chemical weed killers. It is good, too, for irritating things like pebble paths. You can also buy a version which has a hood over it to control the flame, and this will sneak its way very satisfactorily round shrubs. And of course a flame gun is a marvellous lazy bonfire lighter.

But against all this euphoria, flame-guns are sheer hell to heat up – rather like old-fashioned blow lamps before the age of bottled gas. All I can say is that we have, abandoned somewhere in our garage, the "Ezi-use" flame-gun on which we once pinned all our hopes. We seldom if ever got flames; what we had instead was either a loud roar and an uncontrollable blaze, of a sulky hiss and a shower or fuel over our shoes. It also scorched everything that we did not want scorched (including the washing, once, when we pointed it the wrong way to light it). However, you, I'm sure, are not nearly as inefficient as we are, and the flame-gun may be just the right thing for you. You can get one hand-held, or on a wheeled trolly. Hire one, shut up the dog and the cat indoors and see how you get on.

More about machines in general

Every machine, alas, needs caring for. After you've been using it, if you can't or won't hose the mud off the machine right away, wait until it has dried, then knock

Flame-gun for destroying weeds

the mud off; the same goes for matted, tangled grass cuttings clinging to cutter blades.

It's unfortunate but true that you must keep all cutting edges clean, or they simply won't work efficiently the next time round. If you *know* you'll never keep bringing the machine in under cover after use, resign yourself to the situation: buy a proper heavy-duty waterproof cover to fling on it after work is done, and make sure that you anchor it properly, or a sudden gust of wind may blow it away.

A machine will forgive you almost everything except allowing it to run out of lubricating oil. In the small two-stroke engines of the type you get on light mowers, the oil, like that in a scooter engine, comes mixed together with the petrol so there's no worry. But a heftier four-stroke machine needs lubrication frequently. So remember that the dipstick is not just a pretty toy – check the oil level with it each time you use the machine. And remember, the older the machine, the thirstier it gets for lubrication. If you are laying up the machine for the winter, I think it's a good idea to take out the sparking plug and put it somewhere dry. Make sure, too, that the petrol tank cap is screwed firmly on; little bits of grit, rust or even drips of water getting into the tank may make the machine mysteriously pack up, when you are halfway through the lawn.

If your machine won't start, what should you do? First attack the obvious – has it run out of fuel? Have you left the choke out too long, and flooded the carburettor? Walk away leave it for a minute or two, then try to start it again. Are the filters clogged? Take a look and see. If all seems well in those directions, have a good look at the sparking plug. Damp or dirty plugs cause more trouble with small engines than almost anything else. Try a spare one if you've got it, or dry the plug off on the gas stove. Learn to love your machine's little idiosyncracies – I knew a man who had a mower that never started unless he first scribbled on the bottom of the sparking plug with a pencil. He tried to explain to me about the graphite, but I never quite got the message.

Reliable brand names for lawn mowers include: Atco, Qualcast, and Suffolk Iron Foundry. Rotary scythes are made by Landmaster, Qualcast, Suffolk Iron Foundry, and John Allen & Sons. The rotary scythe that works on the hovercraft principle is made by Flymo Ltd.

For cultivators, try Auto-Culto International, Honda, Rotavator and Landmaster Ltd. Tarpet make flexible drive components, hedge-cutters, and electric tillers.

Sprinklers

If you've got the kind of lawn that goes bone dry in summer, leaving you with those embarrassing bald patches, it may pay you to install some sort of automatic watering system.

There are all sorts of sprinklers available, ranging from the type that whirr round of their own accord, covering quite a large area, to the more static kind that act like a fountain.

If on the other hand, it's a flower bed or a vegetable plot that you're worried about, you can install your own home-made sprinkling system without much fuss: Take a length of old hose and perforate it at regular intervals, say every foot, always puncturing it on the same side. Lay it snake fashion on the ground, attach one end to the tap and turn on. (It goes without saying, incidentally, that you don't make your perforations in the pipe too near the tap end!) This makes a perfectly good watering system, provided you don't turn up the water pressure too high, when it may tend to split the pipe.

Remember, by the way, that if you have a sprinkler or a garden hose in constant use you are supposed to tell the local Water Board, as you have to pay extra for it.

7
SCIENCE IS ON YOUR SIDE

THE WAR ON WEEDS AND BUGS

Spray your troubles away. That's the easiest method of keeping the garden tidy and under control. There's something somewhere on sale now for every kind of problem, from weeds in the lawn to greenfly on the roses. But make sure you know exactly what you are doing before you start, and that you've got the product that is going to do what you want it to do.

Make sure, too, that you're doing your spraying at the right time. You must never start spraying anything when there's any wind about, because you've got no control over it at such times. The stuff may be wafted where you don't want it to go – worst of all, it may obliterate the next-door garden, with disastrous and expensive results. So bide your time, choose a moment when the day is sunny, with at most a force 2 wind and – if you're killing weeds – the soil is reasonably damp.

Spraying is not the cheapest way to get rid of weeds. It's only fair to tell you that before you start. The cheapest way to get rid of weeds is to pull them out yourself, with your own two hands. But who wants to spend hours weeding the garden? You end up thinking that nature has got it in for you, personally, as you nurse your aching back. Cheat instead, get science on your side to tackle the job.

Some weed-killers to enlist

There's a useful new weed-killer, Ramrod, produced by Murphy, which is simply scattered on the soil from its puffer pack, and stops weeds before they start.

The cheapest and longest-used weed-killer of the lot, of course, is our old friend sodium chlorate, which you buy in large packets from the chemist. It is a white powder which can be dusted on to the soil or, more safely, mixed with water and sprayed over the ground. It is very efficient and also very ruthless. Any ground that is treated with it cannot be used for growing anything for months – even up to a year, if there hasn't been much rain to wash it away.

Sodium chlorate should, in fact, be called a plant-killer, not a weed-killer, because it will tackle the lot. It's not in the least bit fussy, it will kill off Auntie Minnie's best begonia just as easily as that tuft of couch grass that you've always hated, so it needs treating with with great caution.

It will kill your plants in two ways, by getting at the roots via the soil, and by contact with the stems, and the only way to speed up its work and make the soil ready for cultivation quickly is to flood the ground constantly – which isn't feasible unless you've only treated a small patch. It also has another nasty habit of "leaking" its way from a flower bed on to the grass. Treat it with care.

Sodium chlorate has another nasty habit: spontaneous combustion. A rag soaked in sodium chlorate and left bundled up in a corner may quite suddenly start to smoulder. So be very careful about anything which has come into contact with the stuff, especially clothes.

Children, especially small boys who want to be scientists, have found out that sodium chlorate powder can be employed to make an excellent home-made bomb, so that's another good reason for taking care. It's vital that the stuff is hidden well away, and that your offspring don't know that you have any – though small boys have a way of finding out about these things.

Ammonium sulphamate, which is sold under several different proprietary names, is rather less lethal than sodium chlorate, but does what amounts to the same kind of work. This also kills plants through the roots and the stems, but it is quicker in its effect. You can reckon to replant after a few weeks, rather than months. It is not so effective, however, on the heavy mob like ground elder and bracken, and it's not really strong enough to keep paths permanently free from weed.

Paraquat, which is sold under several names, including Weedol, also kills by contact with the plant, but only works through the greenery, not the roots, and it therefore doesn't do any harm if it soaks into the ground. You can use it to weed between shrubs and things like standard rose bushes, if you are careful with it and dribble it over the offending weeds, making quite sure it doesn't splash your precious plants. It's good, too, for those irritating weeds that come up between the cracks in courtyards and paths. But the beastlier weeds, which have really deep roots and because of this can combat the effect of the paraquat on their leaves, will need more than one dose, in quick succession, to finish them off. If nothing seems to be happening after a few days, give them another going over. It's the sort of job you can knock off in the evening, before it gets dark.

Selective weed-killers are fine for particular purposes. But you want to think very carefully before you dash out and buy them, because you may buy several, quite unnecessarily, when one would do the job. A case in point are those that work on lawns. Some only kill the clover that grows amongst the grass, others will tackle weeds but not clover. Get one weedkiller that will combine both jobs; there are several available. Better still, choose something like Fison's Evergreen, which is a general weed-killer for lawns, mixed with a fertiliser, too, which will do the grass a power of good.

Simazine, which masquerades under several different names, including Weedex, is a weed-killer that clings. It doesn't attack plants through their leaves, but spreads itself over the surface of the ground and gradually sinks in, giving the kiss of death to weed seedlings in the spring and early summer. It takes time to work, and the weeds will begin to flag just about the time when you have given up hope, As it is absorbed through the *roots* of plants, it is not much use on ground that is heavily overgrown with creeping plants which cover the surface – you'll have to roughly hack over or scythe the plants first. Simazine won't take on well-established plants, but just to be on the safe side, it's a good idea to dilute it still further when using it on a flower bed. It is first-rate for paths and patios.

Pests

Greenfly, blackfly, mildew and blight can all be tackled with fungicides and insecticides. The situation is changing so rapidly and there are so many new ones coming on the market, that the best thing to do is to go to your local nurseryman, bearing a piece of the plant, and ask for something to cope with it, or tell him what, specifically, is wrong.

How to do it

Buy yourself a proper sprayer – don't just make do with a watering can, especially if you have a large area to cover. It may seem like an extravagance at first, but it will avoid all that business of mixing things up in pudding basins and bottles and running back for refills.

Most spray packs are plastic, which cuts down considerably on the weight that you have to lug around – the liquid alone is quite enough, thank you. So plastic the container should be, but I prefer anything mechanical

A well-designed sprayer will help you get insecticides where they can do their work

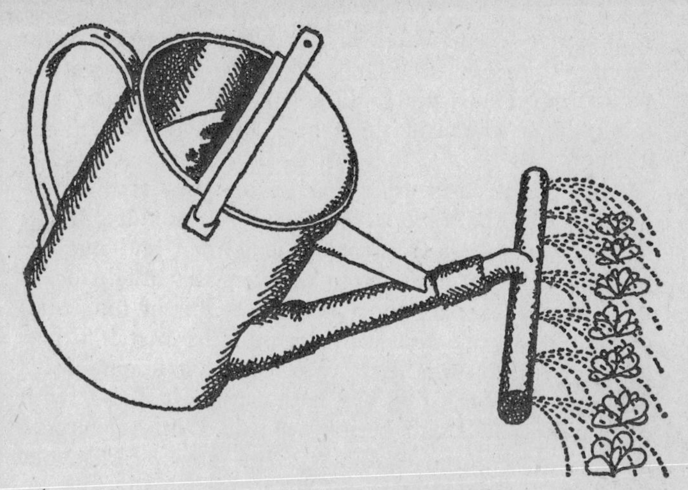

A special sprinkler bar fitted to a watering can ensures that weed-killers go where they should

like triggers, nozzles and so on to be made from metal, because otherwise they have a habit of snapping under strain.

Don't lose your head and buy a king-size sprayer. Remember that even a pint of water weighs well over 1 lb., and it's going to be carried on *your* back. One of the handiest sprayers on sale is the one that you can sling over your shoulder as you walk around. It pays to buy one, if you can, that has a built-in pump which will give you a continuous supply of spray under pressure. But you pays your money and you takes your choice.

The spray goes a long way – remember that, before you start playing with it. It will cover a much larger area than a watering can, so it needs watching accordingly. If you've anything really lethal to infiltrate between plants, you're better off abandoning the sprayer for the moment and using instead a watering can with a drip-bar.

It is not worth while buying a special appliance for dusting things on to plants, but save time by getting your product in a puffer pack which does the next best thing. Most chemical dusts are now available in this form.

After you've been using your sprayer – or your watering can for that matter – wash it out carefully; better still, dump it in a corner of the garden and put the hose in it. Quite apart from disasters that might occur if it's not clean next time you use it, lots of fungicides contain chemicals that can corrode the metal fittings of a spray set. Another way of cleaning it out, if it's difficult to do, is to fill the bath with water and swish it around in it. Don't hesitate to add a little detergent to the water if the container seems greasy inside, but don't use soap powder.

Two awful warnings to end up with: do read the instructions properly before you use any chemicals – it's amazing how many people don't: hospital out-patient departments are full of them. Some chemicals can harm your eyes if you're unlucky enough to splash yourself, so it's a good idea to wear some form of protection – goggles, sunglasses, even an old pair of reading glasses – when using a spray. Some chemicals, ammonium sulphate for instance, must never be used in a metal container or they will corrode it. It says so, quite clearly, on the instructions, but lots of people don't notice – then wonder why the bottom has dropped out of the bucket.

It goes without saying, too, that all insecticides and weed-killers must be kept out of the reach of children. Yet it's surprising the number of people who worry that the pussy-cat might be affected by the fly-spray, and quite forget their own infant child who might find and drink it, thinking it's a bottle of lemonade.

You can't be too careful with poisonous chemicals

8
WHAT PRICE A VEGETABLE GARDEN?

I once grew a lettuce which cost me £2 10s. 0d. (that what's we called it then!) It was the most expensive lettuce I ever had, and quite frankly, it wasn't even up to greengrocer standard, but it was all mine. It was the only one left from a batch of quite expensive seedlings I bought from a nursery, and carefully planted out in the spring. First came the slugs, then a rabbit that had escaped from a neighbour's garden, and between them they demolished the lot, apart from this one precious straggly plant.

When I had calculated the cost of my time, the plants, the expensive fertiliser I had put down, I realised that the wretched thing had cost me more than the price of a dinner for two at our local Indian restaurant.

A too-friendly neighbourhood rabbit is not a hazard that you will necessarily encounter, but this sad story does illustrate only too well one point: don't grow anything that a professional market gardener can do better. If you *must* try your hand at lettuce, for instance, pick something different like the Salad Bowl variety which will – if the slugs allow it to – grow to a size that actually fills a salad bowl. It's less likely to bolt on you, too. Or, if your garden is mainly notable for its splendid crop of dandelions, fling a flower-pot over a plant when it is young, leave it there for 10 days to blanch the leaves,

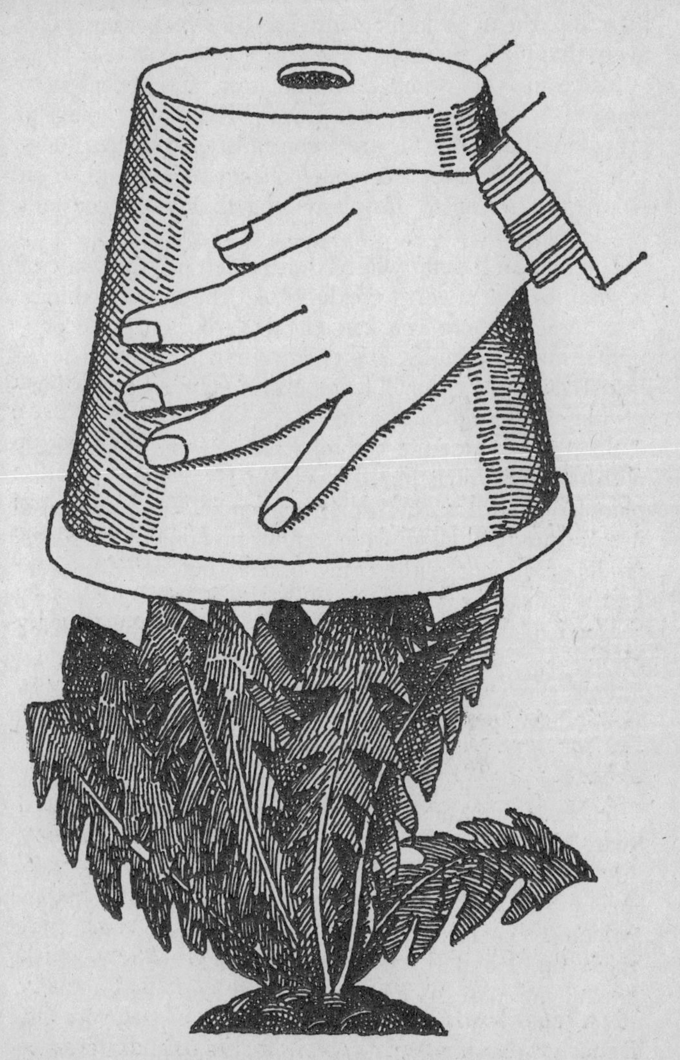

Blanch a dandelion plant by covering it with a pot, and you'll get a useful addition to the salad bowl

then use them as lettuce instead – the blanching takes away that bitter taste.

Make up your mind here and now, and repeat it to yourself when you are tempted: "I am not going to grow anything that I need constantly, in large quantities . . . like potatoes, carrots, cooking onions and so on – nor am I going to grow anything that needs constant loving care."

Having said that, what is there left in the way of vegetables that's worth tackling? All the unusual things. For here is where you can cheat: grow only the one-upmanship vegetables, the ones your friends have never heard about, and they'll assume that your garden is burgeoning with kitchen produce.

So it's out with the common lettuce, and in, instead, with unusual things like Good King Henry, the mercury plant; out with spring onions, sown in succession, and in with the tree onion, which grows tiny onions festooned on its stem; out with spring greens, but in with everlasting kale.

Don't plan a special kitchen garden, either – that's asking for work; just scatter the vegetables instead among the plants. It's heresy, I know, but some vegetables have very decorative leaves and one, the globe artichoke, is actually grown as a garden flower as well. A crown of rhubarb, which is cheap to buy, will look after itself quite happily in the flower bed, year after year. I have some tucked away among flowering shrubs. And if friends shriek, "But isn't that *rhubarb* in your flower bed?" tell them it's actually *Rheum rhaponticum* (which is its formal Latin name), and that will shut them up. Rhubarb, by the way, looks very good set among the more spiky exotic plants, like yucca.

If you want to force rhubarb, incidentally, to give yourself an early crop, simply stick a bottomless box over the plant, or wrap some sacking around the roots. Choose an early variety like "Champagne", then you'll have some ready to eat when it's still expensive in the shops. You buy a crown one year and leave it until the next before you start pulling from it, if you're wise.

What can you have?

Strawberries are *out* for you, unless you grow them for decoration's sake in a barrel. Raspberries are a much better bet, because they are almost inevitably scarcer and more expensive in the shops, and the plants don't need constant replacing. Either of the Mallings – "Malling Promise" or "Malling Exploit" – is good for fruit, and if you mix granulated weed-killer into the soil when you plant the canes, you should have no trouble from weeds.

Growing soft fruit is bound to be a battle with the birds. You can put it all under cages, of course, but these are extremely unsightly and tend to make the garden look like a zoo. There is also a strange, spidery plastic substance you can buy, to tease out and fling over the branches. But it looks like a hideous blight over the tree or bush, and you'll become tired of answering questions about what has gone wrong. Learn to live with the birds instead. Let them have some fruit – you have the rest.

Going back to strawberries, if you're really stuck on growing them, pick the perpetual kind which goes on fruiting all summer until the autumn – you don't want to get a bumper crop just when the fruit's at its cheapest in the shops. The easiest way to keep the birds off strawberries, by the way, is the old-fashioned one – pop a jam-jar over the ripening fruit; it acts as a cloche, too, and brings them on quicker.

A nice close-packed hedge can be used as a host for growing runner beans and peas, but don't whatever you do get involved in erecting bean-poles. Not only do they look frightful, but there is all the problem of taking them down at the end of the season. Beans can be grown up any form of screening you may have in your garden, with very little extra trouble. If you must have sticks, tie them in threes, wigwam fashion – they'll stand up better to the wind that way, and you can grow morning glories up them, too.

A friend of mine (whom many people privately consider to be mad) once grew some runner beans around an old tree. She planted them in a circle round the trunk, then trained them round it in a spiral, using the tree like a maypole. To attach the plants to the tree she used drawing pins and cotton loops, but because a tree takes all the nourishment from the ground around it, she had to dig some manure into the soil around each plant. You can grow runner beans horizontally, too, over netting pegged a few inches above the ground, but this is almost more nuisance to erect than the old-fashioned sticks.

If you're bent on growing beans, skip the old scarlet runner and try instead the golden butter bean (it has nothing to do with butter beans from the grocer, by the way); this is a dwarf plant which sports golden pods instead of the traditional green. The golden butter bean is ready for harvesting before the ordinary kind and you don't have to string the beans, either, they just need topping and tailing before you cook them. Another dwarf bean worth trying is "Tiny Green Snap", which is also stringless, but looks rather more like the scarlet runner than does the butter bean.

The horticulturalists are falling over each other in an attempt to grow bigger and better tomatoes. Let them. *You're* going to grow something different, like the yellow tomato, "Golden Jubilee", which looks lively in a salad (most people mistake it for yellow peppers). I maintain that the yellow tomato even tastes different from the red one, but it's supposed to be the same.

Then there's the Italian plum tomato, which grows in that curious pendulous shape, like the tomatoes you

Easiest way of arranging bean-poles – the wigwam

buy in tins; strictly for fun, and to experiment with, is the grape tomato, which grows in a small bush with fruit like clusters of grapes, and the "Tiny Tim" currant tomato, which you can grow indoors as a pot plant if you want to – it only reaches 18 inches in height and bears surprisingly prolific numbers of tiny fruit.

One woman I know quite deliberately grows green

tomatoes, because all her family love green tomato chutney, so if yours don't ripen, you can always console yourself in this practical way. Never buy a variety of tomato that needs staking. For ordinary purposes "The Amateur" is a good standby – it grows bush fashion and doesn't need the side shoots pinched out. I have even grown tomatoes on the deck of a boat, using "The Amateur" in pots.

Globe artichokes are exotic and surprisingly easy to grow if your soil is good. They make an attractive addition to the flower bed, too – but beware, they take up a good deal of space. Buy them in plant form, and as the heads begin to form, nip off any side-buds if you want large artichokes to eat. You can eat the lower leaves, too, if you blanch them by covering them with earth. If you tire of eating artichokes, let them go on growing, when they will develop into pretty blue flowers.

I defy anyone to tell the difference between a vegetable marrow that has been grown in the garden and one that has come from a supermarket. If you do have an urge to grow anything like that, switch to pumpkins instead. They're more unusual and they make a good pie. Cucumbers are a pretty useless garden crop, now that the market gardeners have got them off practically to a factory industry, but if ordinary cucumbers give you indigestion, it's worthwhile thinking about growing the apple cucumber – it's round and apple-like instead of long. Another cucumber to try if you have a trellis going spare is the Japanese climbing cucumber, which rampages all over the place producing a great deal of fruit.

Ornamental gourds come from the cucumber family, and although of course they're not edible, have a a few for fun; play tricks with their shape by putting the gourd inside a shaped bottle while it is still growing, then breaking the bottle off and letting the plant ripen. If you want to use gourds for decoration, dry them off properly, then polish them with wax to give them a sheen. If you get plants rather than seed they will grow quite happily out of doors – seeds need starting off under glass. Buy them from a specialist nursery.

Horseradish is a useful thing to have around, but it can take over, like ground elder, if you let it go unchecked. The best way to set the "thongs", as the roots are called, is sideways into a minature mountain of well-fertilised soil. Plant them in the spring, and then forget about them until the autumn when you can if you wish take the roots out and store them, or better still, grate them freshly as you want to use them. Go sparingly when you use fresh horseradish if you are only used to the ready-mixed variety – it will bring tears to your eyes as you grate it. Its official name, by the way, is *Armoracia rusticana*.

Asparagus, which costs so much in the shops, is surprisingly easy to grow. All that nonsense that is talked about asparagus beds is unnecessary, unless the soil in your garden is exceptionally sticky and heavy. It's perfectly all right to plant asparagus in the ordinary way. Go to a specialist for the plants and choose the male roots (female plants produce fruit). Plant them in the spring and leave them severely alone for a year. The following spring you can have your first asparagus – you know it's ready when you can see funny brownish-green knobs sticking up for about 2 inches around the crown. Reach down underground and cut off the white stems. In the autumn you just cut the plant back to ground level. It's easy.

Shallots and onion sets are easy to grow – you simply poke the "bulbs" in in the spring, and let them multiply. But keep them well away from your daffodils, or you may, like my poor husband, find yourself accidentally eating fried liver and daffs instead of onion. Shallots should be put in the ground as early in the year as you can ram them into the soil without too much effort.

They need to be 9 inches apart from each other, as they tend to grow sideways, and they're invaluable for some classic French dishes, because their flavour is more subtle than that of onion.

Onion sets are planted in spring, about 6 inches apart in little indentations in the ground. The roots of the onion must be covered with soil, but the bulbs themselves sit on the surface where the sun can get at them to ripen them off.

Despite the apple sawfly, black scab, greenfly and all the other diseases that can attack fruit trees, it's easy enough to include a fruit tree or two in your garden plan. More fun than a straightforward apple or pear tree is one that bears both sets of fruit – you can buy them ready-grafted on to a basic rootstock, and although they've been around for years, they still cause gasps of surprise from the uninitiated. If you've got a dull patch down the bottom of the garden, you could even have a small orchard, with bulbs naturalised in the grass between the trees.

Well worth trying

Now, finally, here's a quick run-down of some of the other way-out varieties of vegetables and fruit for you to try:

Perennial Broccoli (*Brassica oleracea var. botrytis* "Asparagoides") is strictly for the larger garden, as it grows like giant cow parsley, but it's well worth having if you have the room for it. This broccoli produces heads like miniature cauliflowers, as many as a dozen at a time, and at other times of the year you can eat the leaves. The plant needs a reasonably rich soil if it is to do well. Its life-span is about 3 years.

Calabrese also known by the name of Italian broccoli; when you order broccoli spears in most restaurants, this is what they give you, more often than not. It grows green "heads" like cauliflowers on its side shoots. It is an annual, and needs planting out each spring, so you may want to strike it off your list.

Golden Celery: most celery has to be protected from the light while its growing, to preserve those snow-white stems, but not this one. It's self-blanching and therefore ideal for the indolent celery-eater. The ground needs to be fairly rich (celery loves well-rotted lawn mowings). You can buy the plants in June from a nurseryman.

Everlasting Kale: what more could you want for "greens", nursery style? This plant is of the cut-and-come-again kind. It keeps going all the year round and it never bolts. Buy young plants from a nursery – kale will stand any sort of soil. When you cook it, by the way, don't drown it in too much water, and serve it with a knob of butter on the top.

Good King Henry (*Chenopodium bonus-henricus*) is a perennial veg to suit everyone. In some parts of England you can find it growing wild. It has three uses – as a salad vegetable or lettuce substitute in spring, when the leaves are young and tender; as a mock asparagus, when the shoots come through (you can blanch them by covering them with earth if you want to); and, in the case of the larger leaves, as a passable substitute for spinach, without all that grit that spinach seems to attract.

The Tree Onion is happy in any sort of soil, and much easier to grow than the ordinary onion, which can be rather choosy about its surroundings. Buy bulbs in spring, or better still in the autumn, and plant them as if they were daffodils. Soon the shoots will appear, with clusters of little onions on the end. The tree onion can reach a sizeable height. You increase the plants quite simply by nipping off a bulb or two and planting them.

The Welsh Onion is another useful regular which goes on indefinitely. It's more like a chive in its delicate flavour, and it grows clusters of small onions which are very useful in salads. You propagate this one by simply dividing the plant in two.

The Sugar Pea is the one you eat, pods and all, when it's young – the pods don't have the membraneous lining that larger, tougher peas have. Buy the dwarf variety and pick the pods when tiny peas are just appearing inside them.

The Red Brussels Sprout (*Brassica oleracea var. gemmifera* "Rubra") tastes a little like red cabbage and makes a marvellous, colourful addition to an ordinary meal. The plants like a reasonably rich soil, but otherwise once planted out in the open in May they will happily look after themselves. They're particularly good served with cooked whole chestnuts.

Herb facts

A herb garden sounds like a very lovely thing to have; people get all lyrical about the idea of planting herbs in the spokes of wagon wheels or round sundials, but the wretched plants just won't conform. Herbs are, on the whole rather unattractive plants, and some of them, notably mint and dill, will rampage all over the place, strangling the others to death, while varieties like camomile tend to creep about.

By all means keep some perennial herbs in the garden, things like lavender, mint and parsley (which is almost a perennial, but needs replacing after a year or so). But the rest, the more delicate plants, and the ones that are liable to get lost, are better grown in a decent-sized window box, bang outside the kitchen window where you need them. Robert Carrier, the cookery expert does a very useful pack of mixed herb seeds together with cookery cards telling you how to use them – get someone to give you a set for Christmas.

Here are some perennial herbs that it is worthwhile having in the garden:

Alecost (*Costmary*) is used by the French in large

quantities for seasoning and stuffings. Its leaves make a useful livener-up for spring salads. It grows rapidly, and needs dividing every year to keep it under control.

Angelica comes under the fun category; although you can eat the stem, which tastes a little like celery when it is boiled, it is kept mainly for candying and for subsequent use for cake decoration. To candy angelica stems, boil them until soft in a minimum of water (or better still, steam them); peel them when they have cooked, then boil them once again, when they will take on that unreal green shade. Now add an equal weight of caster sugar to the pieces and leave them covered in this for a day or so. Finally boil the whole mixture up again, until the angelica takes on a translucent look, then cover it with granulated sugar and store it until you want to use it.

Balm is useful for flavouring sauces and soups – it has a lemon-like taste. You can also use the leaves in salad. It propagates itself obligingly because it is self-seeding.

Bay: there's only one way to buy this herb and that's in the form of a small standard tree, where it acts as decoration as well. Bay leaves are useful for *bouquets garnis,* for trimming pâté and for use with fish dishes, but be sparing with it.

Borage is not strictly speaking an annual, but this plant self-seeds each year to ensure a continuous supply. The little blue flowers of borage look pretty sprinkled in a salad and have a flavour like gherkins. Plant either in spring or autumn.

Chervil grows rather like Borage, in that it seeds itself. Choose the curly variety, and you can substitute it for parsley as a garnish. Plant it in the autumn or buy small ready-grown plants in the spring.

Curry Plant (*Helichrysum angustifolium*) looks pretty with its silver leaves and yellow flowers and is a particularly useful plant to have to hand, for its leaves do taste like curry and can be used in salads or soups, or dried and kept for seasoning. Buy small ready-grown plants from a herb specialist.

Chives: easy to grow, and useful to have for a light oniony flavour, chives can be used in several ways – the bulbs can be substituted for spring onions (their pungent taste does not linger as long as that of a true onion), the leaves, which look very much like grass, can be snipped and sprinkled over grilled tomato or purée' potato, and the blue-mauve flowers can be eaten in a salad. Buy the bulbs from a nurseryman or beg some from a friend. Force the leaves by putting a jam-jar over them in early spring.

Lavender: scarcely used now for cookery at all, but makes a useful addition to the linen cupboard. Keep it well cut back to stop it straggling; to line a garden path, choose one of the smaller varieties. There's one called "Hidcote" which keeps itself small and bushy.

Fennel goes so well with fish that it's surprising more people don't grow it, for once it is planted in a corner of the garden it will happily go on for years. It likes the sun and a fairly dry soil and, like most herbs, prefers a reasonably rich diet.

Garlic is another herb that's surprisingly pricy in the shops, but easy to grow on the shallot principle: you simply plant a clove or two a couple of inches deep and leave them to multiply. In midsummer, when the leaves turn yellow, rather like a daffodil dying off, lift the bulbs and leave them to dry in the sun. Then take them indoors and store them in bunches in a dry place. You can start your garlic off quite simply by taking a fresh clove or two from your kitchen supply.

Marjoram makes a good flavouring for forcemeats and salads and can be grown quite happily in a pot, as well as out of doors in open ground. A plant will last for several years before it becomes straggly and needs replacing. This is done quite simply by taking cuttings.

Mint will outgrow any weed when it comes to rampaging over a flower bed, so it needs keeping in check. Most people grow spearmint for general kitchen purposes, but black peppermint is stronger and so is pennyroyal. The roots of mint tend to creep and you may find that a new colony has established itself some yards from the parent plant. If you're yanking it out, don't throw it away – hang the leaves and stems up to dry, and they'll be useful when winter comes.

Parsley is a pest to grow, because the seeds take so long to germinate. But if you are in an area where you can't got hold of any, it can be worth your while. Don't bother about drying it, though – you can always get hold of dried parsley, and it's difficult to get exactly the kind of heat that the plant likes to dry it off and at the same time retain the flavour in the leaves. Parsley should be sown in the early summer, or you can buy seedlings for planting in August. It will die down in the winter and reappear in spring. If you want a good supply it's essential to nip off the flower shoots as they appear.

Rosemary is a useful evergreen shrub with pretty blue flowers. The most usual kind is *Rosmarinus officinalis*, which makes a largish bushy plant, but there is a creeping variety, *Rosmarinus officinalis* "Prostratus", which looks good among alpines or on the rockery. Rosemary can be grown easily from cuttings, or by laying the plant (pegging one of the low branches down in the soil and leaving it until it roots), so it's an easy plant to beg from friends.

Sage is good to have around in the garden, if only so that you can make your own real sage and onion stuffing. It's a small, rather woody bush, which likes a little shelter if it is to do really well. Make sure when you are buying that you ask for perennial sage, as there is an annual variety as well.

Savory and Sorrel are two of the rather more unusual herbs which can both be used in savoury sauces, stuffings and stews. You need to buy winter savory – the summer savory is an annual – and to plant it somewhere where the ground is inclined to be poor, because that, strangely enough, is where it thrives the most. Sorrel likes a moist soil. If yours is inclined to be dry, buy French sorrel (*Rumex scutatus*) rather than the English garden variety.

Tarragon is needed as a vital ingredient for real *sauce tartare,* and since it is easy enough to grow, make room for it somewhere. It likes a sheltered corner and a fairly dry soil. (To make tarragon vinegar for *sauce tartare,* incidentally, you simply steep some dry tarragon leaves in wine vinegar overnight, then strain it carefully.)

Thyme is basically an Alpine plant, and as such it does particularly well in stony, gritty parts of the garden where the soil is rather poor, or on a rockery. For use in forcemeats and stuffings choose lemon thyme, which has a slightly sharper flavour.

Some herbs for your window box

Nothing will grow quite so well in a flower pot or a window box as it does in open ground, but for the lazy gardener the sheer convenience of having herbs to hand outweighs the fact that they may not be top quality. A window-box just by the kitchen door, or any sort of container – an old stone sink is good – gives you much more incentive to add herbs to your cooking than if a traipse down to the end of the garden is involved.

Basil, which grows as a perennial in the Mediterranean countries but can't stand our climate, can be sown in a window-box in May, and will grow very quickly. You need it when making sauce for spaghetti and many other Italian dishes.

Caraway is worth growing for its seeds, if you have the patience – you have to sow caraway one summer and wait until the next for your harvest. For this reason it's best to give it a largish pot to itself and to thin out the seedlings when they appear, so that they have about 6 inches breathing space. The seeds, with their distinctive pungent taste, are excellent for cakes and bread.

Dill with its distinctive, aniseed-like flavour, is almost impossible to buy in England. But it's an essential ingredient in many Scandinavian dishes, and enlivens fish up no end. Plant the seeds in the spring, use the feathery leaves in salad and to garnish fish dishes, and when the seeds appear, soak them in vinegar to make the traditional dill vinegar to go with pickled cucumbers.

Marjoram, Borage, Chervil, Chives, Curry Plant, Tarragon and *Thyme* are also useful to have to hand when cooking, and can be grown in a sink or trough. They won't attain the same height and spread that they would left unchecked, but it's so convenient to have them within reach of the kitchen scissors that it doesn't really matter. Another good herb for growing in pots is *Pineapple Sage* (*Salvia rutilans*), which makes a good indoor plant because of its bright red flowers in the winter, and has leaves that are pineapple-flavoured for livening up a salad; try it.

Samuel Dobie & Son of Grosvenor Street, Chester, are suppliers of unusual vegetables; another good source is Thompson & Morgan of Ipswich, though a surprisingly large number of the more off-beat varieties can be found in the general seed catalogues.

Herbs can be obtained from most local nurseries, or may be bought in seed packet form.

9
JUST GOOD FRIENDS
HOW TO CO-OPERATE WITH NATURE

Everybody needs a friend, but nobody more so than the reluctant gardener. Fortunately, there are a number of families of plants that will, if we let them, help us to keep the place looking relatively tidy and *cultivated*; they'll work for us uncomplainingly and kid our friends and neighbours into thinking that we ourselves have been slaving away.

I first met the Russian vine in an outdoor café in Paris. Although the climate was scarcely any better than ours, there out in the open was an overhead trellis of green that looked at first like a grape vine, until I examined the leaves, which had been trained by pruning and tying so that its gnarled branches formed a pattern overhead. The effect was very exotic and very Mediterranean, yet it was happening at temperatures very like those of London.

Now I know that you *can* quite happily grow vines out of doors in England, but they take time, and that's something the lazy gardener hasn't got – he wants quick effects. This is where the Russian vine comes in, for it's just about the fastest growing climber in the book. Give it reasonable soil and it will cover something like 6 feet or more in just one season, and spread tendrils sideways, too. You can let it sprawl all over some unsightly bush or tree, or you can do what the Parisian café-owner

Free-growing climbers like Russian Vine do a fine job of disguising an unsightly shed or garage

did, and train it in time to a passable imitation of a real vine on an outdoor patio.

The Russian vine will act as a ground-cover plant for you, too, it's perfectly happy to choke out any weeds that come in its path, and when its trails of tiny white blossoms come out they made the flower bed look quite pretty. Most garden centres and nurseries sell this useful little plant, which costs about 60p. Its official name is *Polygonum baldschuanicum*, which is quite a mouthful to remember, and it comes from Bokhara. There's another version which is particularly late-flowering, but you won't see any signs of blooms for a while on young plants. When they do come out, however, they are white and pink. This version, which is Japanese in origin, is called *Polygonum multiflorum*.

Call in the *Polygonum* to cover the coal bunker, grow it up a trellis or over an unsightly fence. Eventually you may have to take a hatchet to it to cut down its growth, but if it's an immediate effect that you're after, this is the friend for you.

Want help with the weeding?

Then call in the ground-cover plants and get them to do the job for you. Given time, they will smother all the ground between shrubs, to keep out the weeds, and in many cases provide you with a carpet of pretty flowers, too.

To do the best job, you want carpeting plants which like shade, because that's what they're going to get mainly, when set among shrubs and bushes. I've already mentioned three of them: camomile, raoulia and thyme, but you may want to get away from a grass-like look and have instead a multi-coloured carpet of pinks, whites and blues.

Carpeting plants are so obliging that most of them will even cover well-worn, fagged-out soil for you, especially the kind of ground that you get under well-established bushes and trees whose roots have sucked all the goodness for yards around. They don't even mind some gravel or stones, and you can if you wish, use them to cover an elderly rockery or a low stone wall and turn it into a veritable hanging garden of Babylon.

Alyssum, if it is allowed to roam, makes a perfectly good carpeter, but it is inclined to get tatty-looking in time, though it has one great advantage: it's cheap and easy to find – even Woolworths sell it in the spring-time. It's an annual plant, strictly speaking, but it self-seeds so abundantly that you can treat it like a perennial. The most commonplace variety, the kind you see used as edgings, on window-boxes and in hanging baskets is sweet alyssum (*Alyssum maritimum*), but if you fancy yellow instead of white, pick *Alyssum saxatile* "Citrinum", which is a pale lemon colour; this, incidentally, is a perennial.

Deep-blue lobelia, in its trailing version (*Lobelia tenuior*) is the constant companion of alyssum. Aubrietia, the rock cress is however better at keeping the weeds at bay, and can be found in purples, blues and pinks.

If you've got to cope with a bed that gets a mixture of sun and shade, lay down a carpet of bugle flowers (*Ajuga*) they'll give you good service under either condition, and they spread speedily, too. The easiest variety to get hold of is *Ajuga reptans*, which has blue flower spikes. It is also the one that clings best to the ground and does the work of weeding for you.

The vivid green sandwort (*Arenaria balearica*) from the Mediterranean, will cling to anything, even to large areas of rock. It spreads a tapestry of tiny roots over the surface of the ground, smothering everything in sight, and in early summer it is covered with a shower of tiny white flowers.

For really bad soil, provided that it is not waterlogged, try the New Zealand burr, *Acaena*. Each plant will increase in size by at least 6 inches all round in one season, and several planted near each other will soon close up the ranks to keep out weeds. You can choose between *Acaena buchananii*, which has greyish-coloured leaves, or *Acaena microphylla*, whose foliage is on the bronze side. In the summer *A.microphylla* is covered in dark red flowers that look like clusters of sea-urchins scattered all over the ground.

For truly spectacular foliage – a sea of silver between your shrubs – plant *Chrysanthemum haradjanii*. Its fern-like leaves positively glisten in the sun, and a sunny bed is where this carpeter is happiest. It looks particularly pretty if you plant a handful of miniature bulbs among it, once it has got established.

Another silver carpeter to plant with it is wormwood, (*Artemisia pedemontana*), which also gives you silvery foliage to admire while it gets busy choking the weeds.

Cotula squalida, despite its name, is another good carpeter which will cover 2 feet or more of ground in solid green. Pennyroyal, a member of the mint family (*Mentha pulegium*) makes a first-rate carpeter – with a bonus, as it gives you a constant supply of mint. Flatter and less untidy than spearmint, it spreads rapidly, and as well as lending a hand in the kitchen gives you pretty purple flowers in summer.

I've already talked about thyme, but I can't mention carpeters without recommending one particular variety for polishing off the weeds. It's *Thymus serpyllum*, the kind that grows in a carpet rather than in hummocks, and there are several varieties to choose from, most of them with pinkish flowers, which will spread quickly and make a nice compact, springy ground cover.

During the first year, when your carpeters are settling down into place and beginning to spread, fill up the gaps by sprinkling annual flower-seeds between them, so that you get an all-over look. It's relatively easy to buy a packet or two of easy-growing annuals like clarkia, gypsophila, nasturtium and mignonette, and sprinkle the contents on the soil. Don't take any notice of any nonsense in the instructions about thinning out the seedlings; as they're mingling with carpeters you won't mind if they are crowded and not very tall. The roots of carpeting plants are inclined to be delicate, since they're a fibrous network, so take care when you plant them, spread them out gently with your fingers and untangle them, particularly if they have been pot-grown. Give the plants room to breathe. Take a careful note, too, of the tide-mark where the soil came to when the plant was in the pot; carpeters tend to suffer from claustrophobia and hate being buried too deep – but on the other hand, don't simply plonk them on top of the ground, or their roots will dry out and die.

Two other good places to grow carpeters, incidentally, are between the crevices of nasty concrete tiled terraces, which look bald and uninteresting as they are, and around the edges of fibreglass garden pools to hide the edge. They're good, too, on walls and in window-boxes. And they're simply splendid if you've been left a garden with little or no topsoil, or if you happen to live on rocky land.

Year-round show

Another good group of friends at a rather more showy height belong to the heather family, the *Ericas*, which will also smother weeds – anything that gets out of their clutches deserves to succeed, anyway.

Some heathers positively hate lime soils, but there are several which are quite happy to live with you, whether your soil is chalky, limey or not. The best known and cheapest of these is *Erica carnea* which will good-naturedly take on anything. *Erica carnea* grows fairly low, about 18 inches is as high as it will get, and the two "Springwood" varieties, white and pink, if planted near one another will give you flowers in late winter and early spring. If you want something that will flower in the autumn, pick the variety called "Eileen Porter", which starts off in October and can go on until April, or "Winter Beauty", which begins a little later.

Heathers are definitely a gardener's best friend, because you can organise an all-round-the-year show of colour with their help – there need never be a month when something isn't going on. The only thing that they really dislike is shade, so if your garden has high walls, or is tree-laden, think again. Plant *Ericas* close together and they will soon gang up against the weeds; they'll even take on ground-elder, my arch-enemy.

The true Scottish heather comes under a different family, the lings or *Callunas*, and they must have a lime-free soil. The traditional white heather is *Calluna vulgaris* "Alba", but if you want more of a show, pick *Calluna vulgaris* "H.E.Beale", which has generous pink flowers. Broom (*Genista*) mixes well with heathers and lings and has, for some reason or other, only yellow flowers. You can use one variety, *Genista tinctoria* 'Plena", as a carpeter among heathers and the larger versions of broom with great effect. The most common kind of broom found in the garden is "Mount Etna", which will grow up to 15 feet high as a shrub and looks like a perpetual firework display. It's a good alternative to a tree in a small garden.

In a lightweight soil you could set off a display of heathers with a hedge of common gorse, the kind found in the countryside. Its official name is *Ulex*, and if you are buying some, rather than taking cuttings from wild plants, then ask for the double-flowered gorse, *Ulex europaeus* "Plenus", which does not self-seed – a blessing in this case as gorse is so prolific that it's difficult to keep under control.

If you're running out of cash, incidentally, all the above plants can easily be propagated by taking cuttings – see Chapter 3.

Some of the best garden friends of all are the shrubs

and plants that will give you colour in winter, when the rest of the gardens in the neighbourhood are dank and dripping. It's not difficult to organise at all – many well-known species have their own varieties that flower in the dark, dull months, it's just a case of finding out, first, before you plant. Other plants have attractive coloured leaves that give almost the same effect, yet others have coloured stems and branches, so that when the leaves fall they still look decorative.

If you are hoping for winter flowers on a shrub, give it the best chance you can, and if possible let it have some shelter from the wind. Leave a shrub to shiver alone in an exposed patch of garden, and you're not giving it half a chance.

That great standby, the winter jasmine (*Jasminum nudiflorum*) will give you beautiful gold sprays of colour in the lean months of the year, while *Viburnum fragrans* will keep its end up from November through to March with sweetly scented pink flowers. Another relative, *Viburnum tinus*, more often called Laurustinus, will flower from autumn until spring; if you want white flowers ask for the variety called "French White", while for pink you need "Eva Price".

Daphne mezereum is an old-fashioned plant that has gone out of favour, goodness knows why. Plant the variety called "Grandiflorum" and it will reward you with clusters of sweet-smelling red-pink flowers throughout the winter months.

That old familiar, autumn cherry, *Prunus subhirtella* "Autumnalis", usually comes up trumps right through the winter with delicate white flowers, while *Hamamelis mollis,* the Chinese witch hazel, smothers its leafless branches with yellow stars in the worst weather. If you want a touch of red in the garden, then call in its relation, *Parrotia persica,* which gives you crimson leaves in autumn, then flowers of the same shade in the early months of the year. *Fatsia japonica* is another shrub that is often overlooked, possibly because its leaves look too exotic to be true, but it thrives anywhere, and produces pale green flowers in winter.

Winter foliage is easier to find, for there are no end of trees and shrubs with striking coloured leaves or twigs. They give the garden a bright, jazzed-up look in the darkest months. Take the maple family, for instance; quite apart from the varieties that give you gorgeous colour in autumn, the coral bark maple, *Acer palmatum* "Senkaki", has branches that are a rich coral red in colour, while *Acer griseum*, the paperbark maple from China, has a trunk that peels to show vivid orange-coloured bark beneath.

In the same category comes the Dogwood, *Cornus alba Sibirica*, which when denuded of leaves shows a mass of quite bright red twigs. Or there's *Cornus stolonifera flaviramea,* which has yellow branches.

Silver birches look pretty in winter, too, if you can grow them and they like a fairly sandy soil; try two interesting kinds: *Betula pendula* "Fastigiata", which grows uncannily like a Lombardy Poplar in shape, while *Betula pendula* "Youngii" is a small weeping silver birch. For a different coloured trunk there's *Betula papyrifera kenaica,* which comes from the coast of Alaska and has an orange-tinged bark. All these trees can be obtained from Hilliers of Winchester.

Golden-leaved conifers look wonderful in winter, especially when there's a sprinkling of snow on them. *Thuya occidentalis* "Rheingold" has striking leaves, and only grows to a height of about 6 feet. *Thuya orientalis* "Decussata", on the other hand, has leaves that become almost steel-blue in winter. The climber *Lonicera japonica* "Aureo-reticulata", an almost unknown form of honeysuckle, has variegated leaves which turn a pinkish colour in winter.

Silvery plants make a particularly apt display in the garden around Christmas time – I have even had people

Weeping Silver Birch combines interesting shape and a trunk that looks pleasant during the winter

ask me if I have sprayed a particular bush with silver paint from Woolworths because it looked so bright. There's a version of the homely bramble, *Rubus cockburnianus*, which has silvery stems, but for a really good display, stick to the *Senecios; Senecio laxifolius* is a good silver standby, and so also is a member of another family, *Helichrysum splendidum.*

10
BE YOUR OWN EXTERIOR DECORATOR

It's quite surprising, when you look around you, to see how many gardens are totally inappropriate to the houses they are supposed to partner: Mock-Tudor moderns are paired off with Victorian-style gardens, an ultra-modern house sports a minute plot designed like a scaled-down park round a stately home, and a town terrace house struggles along with a backyard tricked out like a cottage garden, all the annuals wilting sadly in the smog.

It stands to reason that if your house is stark and modern, you need the garden to reflect the idea, with plants and shrubs chosen more for their architectural qualities than for their colour, while a cottage needs a cheerfully messy old-fashioned garden to go with it.

So play exterior decorator – plan your garden around a theme, have some method behind your madness. Be different.

Natural and easy

The easiest kind of country garden to organise is one based purely on grass and bulbs, with a few small trees thrown in to add that extra dimension. They could be fruit trees, too, which would give them an added reason for living.

The essence of a good naturalised garden is that you do not rush out and fling the bulbs whimsically all over

Grass and bulbs make one of the easiest gardens

the place – that way you're laying up a heap of trouble for yourself, and you'll be dismayed at just how many bulbs you need to make a good show. Instead, you plant them in "beds" of long grass, having decided beforehand which part of the lawn you are going to keep short. This means that your garden is designed, your bulbs are crowded together for a showier effect, and you can decide just how much grass you want to mow, and when.

With a natural garden like this, you can rely for colour on the good old steadies, bulbs, corms and tubers, and let the grass grow happily between them. If you want an extra area in which to sit, you simply mow yourself a patch to suit; if you want a path, just run the mower down any part of the garden you fancy. Once the bulbs' foliage has died down, it is quite safe to cut the grass if you want to.

Bulbs will live happily for years without attention, and most of them will multiply, too. They're cheap to buy, because there's so much fierce competition among the bulb-sellers, and if you're cute about it, you can have something flowering all the year round – just organise things so that they come out in suitable succession, for there's no point in having a blaze of colour in the spring, then nothing but green for the rest of the year.

Plant your bulbs in autumn. Naturalise them in the grass – that is, choose a spot, dig a hole in the grass and pop them in. (You'll need the special bulb planter that I talked about earlier, if you're using them on this scale.) If you look down on to your garden, you can scatter the bulbs wherever you like, but if it is going to be almost at eye level, I think they look better planted in clumps. Their only real enemy is mice, who have a particular liking for bulbs if they can get their teeth on them, but you may have some trouble from slugs, too, so it's a good idea when you're planting to sprinkle a little slug bait round the bulbs, for you'd have difficulty in finding them when they are small growing plants.

Here's a calendar of colour for you, a season-by-season flowering guide, based on bulbs and other similar oddments – including rhizomes, from which Irises grow.

SPRING

Daffodils and Narcissus are the mainstay spring flowers in a bulb garden. Officially known as the genus *Narcissus*, daffodils are the ones we all know, with the yellow trumpet flowers. "King Alfred" is the largest, cheapest and most vulgar variety of daffodil, but you can't really beat it for naturalising in grass in large numbers. All the narcissus family are very accommodating, and will grow anywhere – they are not fussy about the soil. "Trousseau" is a pale, pretty daffodil with white outer leaves and a creamy yellow trumpet; for a change try the double narcissus – "Texas", for instance, which looks very pretty with its central ruffle of petals in place of a trumpet.

Miniature daffodils, which reach only about 6 inches tall, look pretty growing in shallow stone pans or in rock gardens. The hoop petticoat daffodil (*Narcissus bulbocodium*) is the most reliable variety to choose, and if you want to replace it by other flowers later on, you can lift the bulbs out *after* the foliage has yellowed and died down – not before, because it is after a plant has flowered and before the leaves die away that it is making new growth down below at bulb level. Dry the bulbs off carefully, not in a damp garage, but in a warmish place like the cupboard under the stairs, and you can then replant them in the window-box or tub early next September.

Tulips (*Tulipa*) tend to stand rather stiffly to attention when naturalised in grass, so if you can only get hold of the most common varieties it is better to give them a miss. But some tulips, notably the parrot type, and the lily-flowered ones, are more feathery and less tailored to look at. And there are double tulips, too. Check the height that the plant is expected to grow to, when buying the corms – some tulips are enormous. "West Point" is a safe kind to choose.

Glory of the Snow (*Chionodoxa*) is an early flowering bulb which will sometimes surprise you by coming out when there is still snow on the ground, giving splashes of brilliant blue flowers in sprays. It's a tiny plant that should be put in clusters under trees, where the grass doesn't grow so long, or it could easily be grown in plant troughs. Its flowers are very like bluebells in appearance, but they have white centres. Chionodoxa self-seeds quite a large area of ground in time, so plant it in a place where it can colonise.

Grape Hyacinths (*Muscari*) also tend to form colonies, and produce spikes of bright blue flowers 6–8 inches in height in early April. They're less formal than the kind of hyacinth that we grow indoors in pots, and they should not be planted too deep – 3 inches is plenty. An even less formal version of the grape hyacinth is *Muscari comosum plumosum*, which has feathery fronds of flowers that wave in the wind.

Spring Snowflake (*Leucojum Vernum*) is one of a family of useful flowers that will, between them, bloom for you right through to late autumn. It produces showers of little bell-like flowers on long slender stems, rather like snowdrops in appearance. It needs planting in the autumn, like most bulbs, and after a year or two you can break up the clusters that have formed around the original bulb to propagate them.

EARLY SUMMER

Snake's Head Fritillary (*Fritillaria meleagris*), despite its rather forbidding name, has very pretty drooping flowers with coloured freckles on them – usually light and dark purple or white and mauve. It grows very fast, and quickly forms large colonies. It usually begins to flower just before the bluebells do, and looks very good mixed in with them. Plant the bulbs in September, about 4 inches deep. Fritillaries like a damp spot to live in, if you can find them one.

Bluebells (*scilla*) will form colonies of colour for you, and go particularly well in a woodland setting. If you want them to come king-sized rather than like the wild ones, ask your nurseryman for the Spanish bluebell, which is larger than our own home-grown variety. You can also ring the changes and plant pink bluebells and white ones, too, in the same variety, *Scilla hispanica*.

Snake's Head Fritillary comes in early summer

Plant them fairly deep in the autumn (about 5 inches is right), then leave them to get on with it.

Fair Maids (*Ranunculi*) are related to the buttercup and grow just as vigorously. Their flowers look very similar, too, except for *Ranunculus Aconitifolius*, which is white, and can be bought in either single or double-flowered versions. Fair maids flower in May and, like their more ordinary cousin the buttercup, prefer damp places. They grow from tubers instead of bulbs, but should generally be planted in the autumn in the same way.

The Greek Windflower (*Anemone blanda*) is nothing like our old friend the anemone that you see in the florist's, but a plant that produces delicate daisy-like flowers. It's fragile-looking, but a good friend to have, for it will stand even a poor, dry soil, though, having come from Greece originally, it does like its sunlight, so don't plant it under the shade of trees. It's not very tall – it only grows to between 4 and 6 inches in height. If you are energetic you can split the clumps up after a year or so and give yourself a bonus by planting a new colony elsewhere.

Alliums are relatives of the onion – just sniff them to check – but although they may not have a pleasant scent about them, they produce useful flowers for a bulb garden. One particular kind, *Allium karataviense*, has large, close-packed flower heads that look rather like pink dandelion clocks. It flowers in late May, when the more showy spring flowers have died down. Two taller varieties are *Allium rosenbachianum*, which has similar flowers in a purply colour, and *Allium moly*, which has flowers of bright yellow. All three look good mixed together.

Lily of the Valley (*Convallaria masalis*) loves the shade, and that's the best place to plant it, really, as it doesn't look particularly pretty when it's growing, with its stiff green protecting sheath. But it's worth having, if only for its fragrant scent, and to cut the flowers for indoor use. Lilies of the valley are notorious for spreading with great speed, so if you plant a few you'll quickly find you have a large family.

MIDSUMMER

The Summer Snowflake (*Leucojum aestivum*) has slightly larger flowers than the spring snowflake, but for all that it still looks very much like a snowdrop. It grows about 18 inches tall, and like the spring variety, should be planted in the autumn.

Montbretia is almost like a smaller, finer version of the gladiolus, with its orange-red flowers on slender spikes. It's very hardy, accepting almost any soil that you give it, however poor, and it's useful because it flowers in August and early September. Plant in the spring, about 2 inches deep, and try to give it a spot with plenty of sun.

The Summer Hyacinth (*Galtonia candicans*) has pretty little bell-like flowers that droop from tall stems, towering above the grass, with an elusive pleasant perfume. Plant summer hyacinths in the spring, about 5–6 inches deep; they don't take kindly to a poor soil and need to be in the sun.

St Bruno's Lily (*Paradisea liliastrum*) blooms in June and July, giving you a shower of tiny lily-like flowers. It needs a moist soil, so grow it at the bottom rather than at the top of a slope.

AUTUMN

Nerines are the more exotic South African cousins of the daffodil, though you'd never think so, for they look more like lilies. If you can get them to flower – for they like a warm spot – they will reward you with some fantastic blooms to cut and bring into the house, and to make your neighbours positively green with envy. Once happily established, they will form colonies, and they hate being disturbed. *Nerine bowdenii* is the variety to choose; it has wonderful feathery pink flowers on stiff, upright stems, which come out in September, before the leaves show. Plant Nerines in the autumn like other bulbs.

Snowdrops (*Galanthus*). There is, surprise, surprise, a kind of snowdrop which flowers in late September, just when everything else is beginning to look a little sorry for itself. The autumn-flowering snowdrop is best bought in the form of tiny plants rather than bulbs, and you need to settle these in during the autumn ready for flowering next year. *Galanthus "Reginae Olgae" is* an autumn-flowering variety that grows well in grass.

Autumn Crocus (*Colchicum*) is not really a crocus at all, though it looks exactly like one. The only difference is that the flower comes out before the leaves do, and the bulb from which it grows is much larger than that of the ordinary crocus – but it's real enough to make friends do a classic double-take when they see it growing in your garden. *Colchicums* are usually mauve and white and will naturalise in grass with fairly good grace, though they prefer to queen it instead in a flower bed. There are also some common *crocuses* that will, obligingly, come out in the autumn for you, but they are inclined to be smallish and fragile. *Crocus speciosus,* for instance, blooms in September; it needs planting in early summer.

Autumn Snowflake (*Leucojum autumnale*) is the latest flowering of all the snowflake family and gives you pink-tinged flowerlets instead of plain white ones. It needs planting in late summer ready for next year. Mixed with the autumn crocus, it gives a convincing look of early spring to a flower bed or under a tree.

Autumn Daffodils (*Sternbergia lutea*) despite their name, look very much like large crocuses. They are smallish, rather shy flowers with long, thin, grass-like leaves to them, and they bloom in late September and October – through to November, too, if you are lucky. Coming

Nerines make a good autumn show, if they like your garden

originally from the Middle East, they are partial to plenty of sun, and may not reward you with flowers unless they get it.

WINTER

The Winter Aconite (*Eranthis*) is a cheerful little plant for the grey days of January. It has yellow flowers that look rather like buttercups, with fringed foliage, and it stays quite small. You can plant the winter aconite quite safely in the shade and it will cope with any kind of soil.

Bulbocodium vernum is a useful little Alpine bulb to grow with the snowdrops and the crocuses. It has feathery flowers in a pretty pinky-blue shade. Plant its bulbs slightly deeper than you would daffodils, and divide them up after a year or so, when the flowers begin to look overcrowded and clumpy.

Snowdrops (*Galanthus*) can come to the rescue right through winter – *Galanthus corcyrensis* will turn up trumps and flower in November, and *Galanthus silicicus* puts in an appearance in December. The ordinary snowdrop is *Galanthus nivalis*, but if you want something taller, get *Galanthus elwesii,* which gives a bolder display of flowers and leaves. Snowdrops tend to get clumpy in time, but you can always divide them up when they have finished flowering and the leaves have died off, and start a new colony elsewhere.

Crocuses give a bright blaze of colour that the birds certainly appreciate – at least they always have a go at the petals of mine. If you are naturalising them, plant them in clumps or the flowers may become hidden in the grass. For really vivid yellow flowers try "Goldilocks", or get *tomasinianus* if you prefer a pinker hue. Plant the bulbs in September, then sit back and wait.

Two final observations on bulbs – don't plant them under evergreen trees, particularly low-growing conifers, or they'll starve the plants of the light that they need. And if someone, mistakenly thinking you like gardening, gives you some bulbs in a pot, don't throw them away after they have flowered. It doesn't take any longer just to pop them into the ground instead, and if they haven't been forced too furiously, they might just come up again next year.

The colour theme

Another idea you might like to try, especially if you have a rather new house and a rather nondescript plot of ground that needs something done about it, is the colour-co-ordinated garden, with beds of all reds and oranges, of blue flowers and unusual green foliage or even, for a small plot, a one-colour garden.

Vita Sackville-West, the only author I've found who made gardening books compulsive reading, has left a wonderful all-silver garden at her home at Sissinghurst Castle. It's an idea that you could easily copy, and which looks particularly good in town.

You have to cheat a little, of course, by using some plants that are whitish rather than silver, but you can even start with privet in a silvery colour – *Ligustrum Lucidum* "Excelsum superbum" has leaves that are variegated with silvery white, and *Ligustrum sinsense variegatum* is soft grey-green with white flowers, while *Lamium galeobdolon,* a relative of the Dead Nettle, makes a silvery carpeting plant. Many varieties of Artemisia are silver: *Artemisia ludovciana* makes a good bushy plant, while *Artemisia pedemontana* turns itself into a thick silver mat.

Then there are the furry silvery-leaved plants like rabbit's ear (*Stachys*) and white perennials like gypsophila and achillea, which have some silver-grey-leaved varieties. And for show, get the thistle-like Sea Holly (*Eryngium*), with stiff silver-blue leaves and blue-silver flower heads.

An all-gold garden would be just as easy to organise, using lemon-gold flowers wherever possible. Here the golden privet (*Ligustrum ovalifolium* "Areo-Marginatum") would look perfectly respectable as a basic background or you could have one of the golden cypresses – there are silvery ones, too. Broom and golden rod would go well in a yellow-gold garden, so would golden grass (*Milium effusum aureum* "Mr Bowles"). Ideas like this are inclined to arouse feelings of "Why ever didn't *I* think of that?' in the most devoted gardeners' breasts.

Exotic terrace

If you're reduced mainly to a patio, you can give it a Mediterranean look. Instead of planting the true Italian cypress, which does not always take kindly to this climate, you could stick to *Chamaecyparis lawsoniana* "Columnaris", which makes a perfect slender shape and grows more fast and more vigorously over here. Then, when summer comes, you could add geraniums and other typically Mediterranean plants in special tubs or beds.

11
SOME MORE DESIGN IDEAS

Cottage gardens are meant to look artlessly untidy, a delightful sprawl of different plants, cheek by jowl with each other. The catch is they need to be based mainly on annuals, which makes them a nuisance to cope with, and require a helluva lot of weeding.

If you've got the kind of house that cries out for a cottage garden, the thing to do is to give the *impression* of a traditional old-fashioned plot without all the work. In other words, a picture of organised disarray, but using only perennials, and substituting one amenable plant for its less accommodating relative.

The basis of all cottage gardens is the flower border. But if you're not going to give yourself a lot of unnecessary work, you'll choose dwarf plants, whenever possible, instead of their more usual taller types – even that old standby golden rod comes in a dwarf version now. If you want to have really tall plants up against the fence, traditional things like delphiniums, cut down on staking by running across a few wires parallel to the fence itself, and persuade the plants to use that. And in between the medium-sized plants you can have appropriate ground-covering plants like the evergreen kind of honeysuckle and the pretty little periwinkle, which will keep the weeds down. Elsewhere let mint and thyme run rampant (after all, they're useful in the kitchen, too).

'... a delightful sprawl of different plants ...'

Planning a cottage garden

You'll need delphiniums and lupins instead of larkspur, which has to be sown every year, the everlasting pea instead of the annual sweet pea. You'll choose pinks instead of carnations (which really need a greenhouse) and coral bells instead of Canterbury bells, which need sowing every autumn. And you'll have to pass up stocks and sweet williams, marigolds, too, though you may be tempted to sow some nasturtiums to cover the rubbish heap, because they grow so very easily.

Don't forget the daisies to help you get that cottagy look; there are lots of obliging plants with daisy-like flowers which will look after themselves happily and give you a good display of colour. Plant for instance, fleabane (otherwise known as *Erigeron*), which mixes well with Michaelmas daisies and looks very much like them. You can get it in pinks, blues and mauves, and a hybrid plant in soft orange. The purple cone-flower (*Echinacea*), despite its name has flowers resembling daisies, and is a good choice for the back of the border, as it grows 4 feet high or more. Another back-of-the-border plant is rudbeckia, which is sometimes called "Black-eyed Susan", while gaillardia, yet another daisy-like plant, has flowers that are shaded like anemones. Daisy-like chrysanthemums, which are a far cry from the greenhouse monsters you buy by the bunch, make good border flowers, especially *Chrysanthemum maximum* the big white moon or shasta daisy.

By adding a few more daisy-like flowers, like for instance *Anthemis tinctoria*, the golden marguerite, and some heleniums, you could have a whole daisy border, using the real daisy, *Bellis* "Dresden China" (the pink-tipped form) as a ground-cover plant between them.

Don't forget the favourite old flowers like hollyhocks; you'll find them listed in catalogues under their formal name *Althaea*. They're plants to put well back where they have something to lean against, because they'll grow 6 feet high, but they'll reward you for your trouble with bright spikes of flowers in single or double form. They mix well with the perennial sunflower, *Helianthus* – choose the "Monarch" sunflower for height, "Loddon Gold" for its bright double golden flowers. You can buy dwarf versions of the sunflower, too, but they don't somehow seem the same.

Foxgloves, gypsophila and lobelias all come in both annual and perennial forms, so be careful which kind you get. The perennial gypsophila has smaller flowers than its sister, but *vive la différence* so far as work is concerned! *Gypsophila paniculata* makes a handsome plant some 2–3 feet high, with pretty white flowers, and can be grown from cuttings. The perennial foxglove with pinky-white flowers, is called *Digitalis mertonensis*. Another taller perennial version is *Digitalis ambigua*, which has creamy-white flowers. Perennial lobelias are usually red rather than the blue of the annual variety, but *Lobelia vedrariensis* will give you the usual deep blue flowers.

Some real old "granny" flowers for the border are leopard's bane (*Doronicum*), a bright yellow daisy (stick to *Doronicum caucasicum* "Magnificum" which is the shortest type), and bleeding heart (*Dicentra*) – this is also called lucky locket in some parts of the country, because it has flowers like heart-shaped lockets that are red on the outside, white within; *Dicentra eximea* is the smaller version of this particular plant. Goat's beard (*Aruncus*), another granny plant, loves the damp and doesn't mind what kind of soil it has, or even if it is in the shade, provided it has plenty to drink. It grows anything up to 6 feet tall, with sprays of white flowers. Granny bonnets or columbines are sold under the official name of *Aquilegia*, and make pretty self-seeding flowers for the border. You don't have to buy them in blue – you can get them with purple, red white or yellow flowers as well, and they grow around 2 feet tall.

Phlox is a very cottagy if rather untidy perennial plant. There are hundreds of varieties to choose from, but make sure you stipulate a perennial plant, or you may find yourself phlox-less again when the year ends. One of my favourites is "Graf Zeppelin", which fixes you with beady red eyes from the centre of white petals. Phloxes will do quite well in the shade if you want to put them there.

Don't forget a few other old-fashioned flowers with real old country names – lamb's ears (*Stachys*) for instance, with furry grey leaves that children like to stroke, and purple flowers; Jacob's ladder (*Polemonium*), which has laddered fern-like leaves and blue-whitish flowers. Then there's Solomon's seal (*Polygonatum*), with graceful, large, bell-shaped flowers on curving stems.

When winter comes there's the Christmas rose (*Helleborus niger*), with beautiful white flowers like giant buttercups in shape, followed by the Lenten rose (*Helleborus orientalis*), which comes out in January and goes on until March. And here of course you can bring in the bulbs . . . snowdrops, crocuses and dwarf daffodils.

Soft fruit and herbs will mix in beautifully with a cottage garden. It's easy to slip in a few gooseberry and currant bushes, for instance, among the larger flowering perennials. A cousin of the edible currant – the flowering currant (*Ribes*) produces trails of pink or carmine flowers, even if it does not give you fruit, and can be planted to make a delightful cottage hedge.

Old English lavender is a must in a cottage garden, but it can become rather straggly in time, so if you want to try a smaller, more compact version, buy *Lavandula stoechas*, which comes from the South of France, or "Hidcote", which has very deep purple-blue flowers. Instead of the ordinary rather bushy rosemary, you could plant Jessup's Upright in the back of the border – it will grow as tall as you are within a couple of years.

For winter decoration indoors don't forget three good old cottage flowers: statice (*Limonium*), otherwise known as sea lavender, with spiky blue flowers you can cut and dry indoors for flower decoration; Chinese lanterns (*Physalis franchetii*), which has uninteresting off-white flowers but gorgeous lantern-like seed pods in deep orange that you can dry off, and finally good old honesty (*Lunaria*) which has a show of bright purple flowers in early summer, then those well-known flat pods that are the same purple colour at first, but later turn silver, with a paper-like feel about them.

A quick run-down of the flowers to choose for a cottage garden, and the positions in the border in which they should go, appears below. Don't forget, by the way, that an island border of cottage flowers is particularly effective, with the tallest plants in the middle and the smaller ones at the sides and either side.

For the Back of the Border

Hollyhocks (*Althaea*)
Goat's Beard (*Aruncus*)
Michaelmas Daisies (*Aster*)
Delphiniums
Red Hot Pokers (*Kniphofia*)
Foxtail Lilies (*Eremurus*)
Heleniums
Sunflowers (*Helianthus*)
Heliopsis
Lupins (*Lupinus*)
Phlox
Rudbeckias
Golden Rod (*Solidago*)

For the Centre

Marguerites (*Anthemis*)
Colombines (*Aquilegia*)
Campanulas
Korean Chrysanthemums
Bleeding Heart (*Dicentra*)
Leopards' Bane (*Doronicum*)
Erigeron
Everlasting Pea (*Lathyrus*)
Stachys
Gaillardias
Gypsophila
Statice (*Limonium*)
Lobelias
Poppies (*Papaver*)
Peonies (*Paeonia*)
Chinese Lanterns (*Physalis franchetii*)
Jacob's Ladder (*Polemonium*)
Dwarf Golden Rod (*Solidago* "Wendy")

For the Front

Small Columbines (*Aquilegia*)
Dwarf Michaelmas Daisies (*Aster*)
Hellebores (*Helleborus*)
Forget-me-nots (*Myosotis*)

For Edgings and Ground Cover

Thrift (*Armeria*)
Pinks (*Dianthus*)
Periwinkle (*Vinca*)
Evergreen Honeysuckle (*Lonicera giraldii*)

For Hedgings

Rambling Rose
Hawthorn (*Crataegus*)
Flowering Currant (*Ribes*)
Hardy Fuchsia (*Fuchsia magellanica*)

The sophisticated touch

Go exotic, choose plants with some tropical allusion about them, if you've got a modern house with rather stark lines about it. It gives a one-up look to an ordinary suburban garden, and those plants which are generally rather tailored and architectural in their appeal blend in beautifully with the simple look.

I've already mentioned bamboos and pampas grass as good showy plants for an island bed. And it goes without saying that they mix well with tropical-type plants, but don't be tempted into sticking them in a corner, where they will simply look messy. Give them pride of place on their own.

The Chilean Gum Tree (*Escallonia*) is an exotic evergreen shrub with shiny leaves and pretty sprays of pink flowers. Much more a bush than a tree, it can occasionally surprise you, if it likes your garden, by shooting up to 7 feet or more in height. As it's South American in origin, it is inclined to be choosy about the climate, but two varieties that are safe are *Escallonia langleyensis*, with dark pink flowers, and *Escallonia x edinensis*, with flowers of paler pink. You could use the Chilean gum tree to make an exotic hedge for a modern garden, if you kept its top cropped; it you're planning it for this purpose you're better served by the variety *macrantha*, which has near-crimson flowers, or "Gwendolyn Anley", which is dwarf-sized by nature.

Hibiscus, despite its South Sea island connotation, can quite happily be grown in Britain if you choose *Hibiscus syriacus*, the hardy variety. It goes on flowering at a useful time autumn and gives you sprays rather like those of the hollyhock in shape, in blue-purple or red. It needs a sunny position, when it will reach 6 feet or more.

Yucca gloriosa, which comes from the Mexican desert, is a spiky plant which looks at first sight just like the head of one of those rather stubby palm trees you find

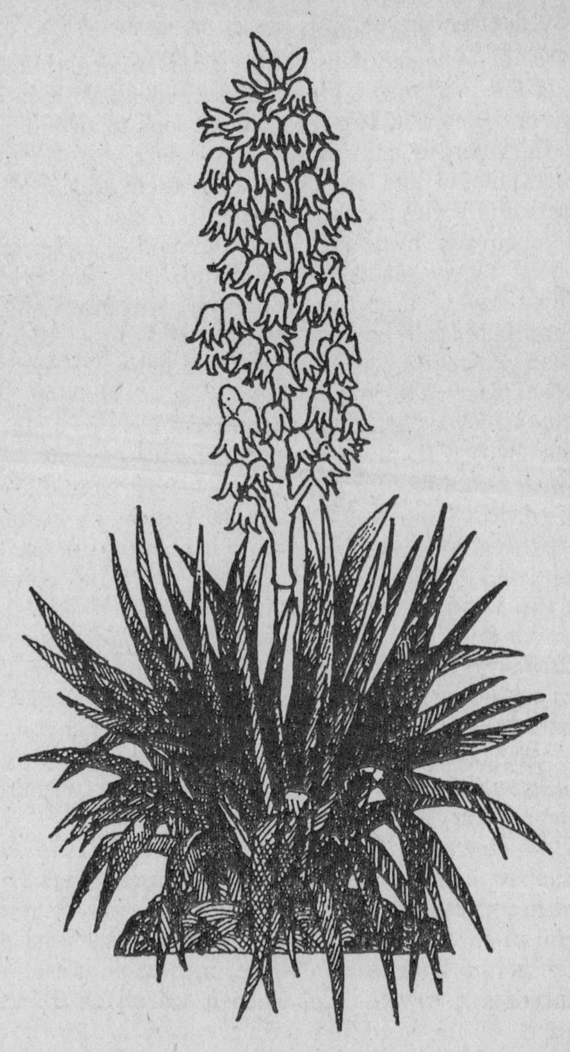

Yucca has handsome leaves, even when there's no imposing flower spike in evidence

in Mediterranean cities. It has an attractive shape, with its sword-like leaves, and it is an evergreen, too. It throws up spikes of whitish flowers in midsummer. But you can't be absolutely sure that it will flower every year without fail, sometimes it sulks. However, it's worth having in the garden, for all that, because of its tropical-looking leaves alone.

The Chusan Palm (*Trachycarpus fortunei*) copes perfectly well with the climate anywhere in the South of England, and very often in the Midlands and the North, too, if it is given some shelter. It's a slow grower, but fun to have in an exotic garden, with its distinctive palm leaves which fan out anything up to 3½ feet wide. The Chusan palm is an evergreen, too, and can in time grow to 15 feet or more.

The Tasmanian Eucalyptus (*Eucalyptus Gunnii*) is one of the toughest kinds of the eucalyptus tree, with its blue-green leaves and distinctive smell. It needs cutting back in spring if it makes too much spindly growth, for it doesn't stand up to gale-force winds very well.

The Tree Peony (*Paeonia suffruticosa*) is really more of an exotic shrub than a tree. It likes a place that gives it shelter from late frosts, when it is forming new growth for the year, but is worth growing for its generous, peony-like flowers in purple, white or all the pinks. There are also yellow species and hybrids.

The Siberian Crab (*Malus x robusta*) has in spring a shower of pale pink flowers, just like almond blossom, and in autumn yellow cherry-like berries on its branches. It keeps its fruit right until Christmas, unless you want to pick it and use it for making crab-apple jelly.

Moroccan Broom (*Cytisus battandieri*) is an exotic version of the good old ordinary wild broom, but its leaves look more like those from a laburnum tree. It will give you a firework display of yellow flowers, with a scent like pineapple about them, all through the summer, and if you plant it by a sheltering wall it can reach considerable heights.

Chilean Barberry (*Berberis darwinii*) gives you little sprays of orange flowers on spikes of glossy dark green leaves, then, later on, purple-black berries. (It's called after Charles Darwin, incidentally, because he first found it in its native Chile.) It's a good-looking bush that is capable of looking after itself without any pruning.

Camellias frighten people into thinking that they are hot-house plants. It's true that an early frost may spoil the first flowers, and therefore it's sensible to put the plants somewhere fairly sheltered, but they are in fact perfectly sturdy. Camellias like a peaty soil if they can get it, but they will grow anywhere as long as there is not too much lime in the soil. And even then you can get round the problem by planting them in tubs. *Camellia japonica* in both versions, with single or double flowers, is the best-known and the sturdiest kind. It grows slowly, but in time can end up as a 10-foot high bush.

Japanese Quince (*Chaenomeles*) flowers in the spring and gives an exotic look that will knock the more ordinary almond and cherry blossoms for six. The showiest variety is "Knaphill Scarlet", with clusters of vivid orange-scarlet, cup-like flowers surrounded by small waxy-green leaves. There are several dwarf quinces, too, for small gardens – *Chaenomeles superba* "Simonii" is one, with blood-red flowers; *Chaenomeles japonica alpina* is even smaller, with clusters of orange flowers.

Mexican Orange Blossom (*Choisya ternata*) has starry, white, sweetly scented flowers all through late spring and early summer. It is a bush that will take on any soil, even chalk, but it hates intense cold, so if you live in a nippy part of the country, forget it. It's an evergreen, with those waxy leaves that give it a tropical look.

Chinese Privet (*Ligustrum Lucidum*) – privet was

never like this! You can hardly believe that it belongs to the same family. It's an evergreen that will grow into a handsome tree if you want it to, or shape itself into a hedge or a bush. The dark green leaves carry a plethora of creamy flowers in the autumn. Another exotic privet, *Ligustrum japonicum*, has smaller leaves, rather like those on the camellia, and white sprays of flowers.

Japanese Maples (*Acer japonicum* and *Acer palmatum*) look most exotic grown by themselves as so-called specimen trees. True to their origin, they seem to grow into particularly aesthetic shapes and in autumn the colour of their leaves is so vivid that they seem to be burning. *Acer palmatum* "Atro-purpeum" has the best colour through the year (though others are more brilliant in the autumn) and it grows quite quickly into a respectable size. *Acer palmatum* "Senkaki" is the Coral bark maple, which has rich red branches in winter, but a less elegant shape.

Magnolias fit well into an exotic garden. For a showy position choose *Magnolia denudata*, the Yulan tree, or *Magnolia x soulangeana,* with pink-white flowers. They're both deciduous, unfortunately and inclined to be slow-growing, but when they do decide to flower they give a wonderful show. *Magnolia grandiflora*, the evergreen magnolia, is the one that I am blessed with. It has leaves that look suspiciously like laurel – in fact it is called the laurel magnolia in some catalogues. It is not a tree that I would recommend heartily, except to be put among other shrubs. Mine is 18 feet high and grows right by the front door. It is evergreen all right, but from time to time during the year it rains down large brown leaves all over the step. It has another irritating habit: when the leaves rustle in the wind they make it sound as if it is raining. It also tends to sulk, and only flowers once every two years or so, but it *is* on a north-facing wall.

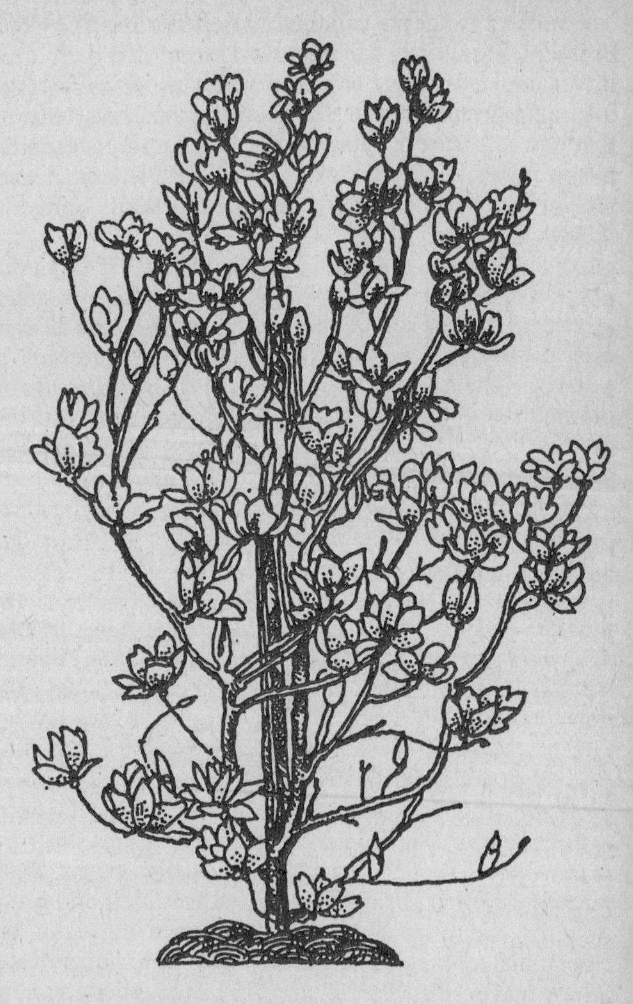

Magnolias have wonderfully exotic-looking flowers

Acanthus (sometimes called rather insultingly, Bear's Breeches) is another exotic-looking plant with dark green leaves and tall lupiny spikes of purple flowers. It comes originally from Greece and makes a good partner for the yucca. Acanthus grows about 4 feet tall. If you want purple flowers, order *Acanthus spinosus*; if you want pink or white, *Acanthus mollis*.

Japanese Snowflower (*Deutzia*) will give you what gardening catalogues call a "good show". It's a bushy plant that is showered with clusters of flowers from early summer on, and there are endless colours and varieties to choose from. The double-flowered variety looks, to myopic me, like a rose bush when it is in full spate. The only snag with the Japanese snowflower is that it sheds its leaves in autumn, so you're left with a sad-looking bunch of twigs through the winter.

Azaleas and *Rhododendrons* go well in an exotic garden and need very little attention. They loathe lime and love acid soils, but will grow happily in one that is reasonably well balanced, and flower anywhere except in deep shade. It's a good idea to plant azaleas in front of the rhododendrons which tower attractively behind them, for the latter tend to get rather stringy-looking round the base as they grow high, and the dwarf azaleas hide the deficiency. Don't make the mistake of buying a deciduous azalea – stick to the evergreens, and go to a specialist for your plants. There is a huge selection now available, ranging from tiny alpine ones to huge trees. Azaleas may be propagated by cuttings and rhododendrons by layering – both are quite easy to do if you start them off in early summer.

The Wig Tree (*Cotinus coggygria*) isn't really a tree at all, but a huge bush which reaches 6 feet high or more. It is grown for its incredible flowers, like small feather boas, which start off a salmonish pink and change to grey later on, when they look like an old man's beard. The wig tree needs plenty of room for its branches to spread. Plant it by itself and you'll see how it got its name – it wears what looks like a wig of flowers. Some varieties, the *Cotinus coggygria* "Foliis purpureis", for instance, have leaves which turn red in the autumn.

The Mexican Tiger-Flower (*Tigridia*) is grown from bulbs and has flowers with petals shaped rather like tulips but striped with fantastic colours of orange, yellow and red. It can be brought indoors and used as a pot plant if you wish, otherwise it is quite happy in a border.

Sea Holly (*Eryngium*) looks like an exotic version of the traditional Scottish thistle, standing up stiffly with silvery leaves and stems and huge bristly flower cones. *Eryngium* "Oliverianum" grows about 3½ feet tall and has blue flower heads, *Eryngium planum* is shorter, with deeper blue flowers. They look their best grown against a background of evergreens or a fence.

The Red Hot Poker (*Kniphofia*) looks marvellous mixed with Sea Holly. The variety that lives up best to its name is *Kniphoffia uvaria*, which has spikes graduating from yellow to red and grows about 4 feet tall. "Mount Etna" is the tallest version of the lot, but its spikes are almost all red.

Balloon Flower (*Platycodon*) has buds that look just like miniature balloons hanging on its branches. Later they explode into bell-like flowers. It goes down well in an exotic garden; for border use stick to the dwarf variety, *P. grandiflorum* "Apoyama", which grows to 6–8 inches and it grows less than 1 foot, needs no staking.

Shooting Stars (*Dodecatheon*) is strictly speaking, a rock plant. It has showers of stripy pink and white or mauve and white flowers grouped on a tall stem, just like sparklers, and it will grow happily under trees.

The Opium Poppy (*Papaver somniferum*) is a nuisance because it's an annual and you need to grow it from seed. But if you can be bothered to do so, it will reward you with fantastic double flowers in rich reds

Sea Holly is unusual in both flower and foliage

and purples and then afterwards with huge, heavy seed heads which are often used for flower decoration. It looks good planted among pampas.

A fine source for trees and shrubs, especially the more unusual and exotic ones, is Hillier & Sons of Winchester. They can even provide you with almost fully-grown specimens for an instant garden – at a price. Write for their catalogue, specifying the plants in which you are interested; there is a small charge for some Hilliers catalogues, but they are well worth having.

12
PORTABLE GARDENS

INDOOR AND OUTDOOR GARDENING EXPERIMENTS

So you've succeeded in concreting almost all of the garden, or you've gone one better and moved into a flat with nothing more than a patio to go with it! And surprise, surprise, you're beginning to miss the greenery. The answer's simple: pick yourself some plants that you can move around, growing them in pots and tubs.

Almost anything, even a small tree, will grow in a container if it's properly looked after and has the right soil, but if you're going to all that trouble, you might as well make it something special.

The art of container gardening

The first lesson to learn is to make your container easily *movable,* if it is of any size at all. Wooden tubs can be made quite simply with castors on the base – use the heaviest castors you can get; heavy concrete pots are much easier to shift if you put an unobtrusive piece of plastic mesh or sacking under them, with enough left sticking out for you to be able to pull on it. Or you can take the easy way out and grow your plants in a wheelbarrow, or do as I do and pile up the flower pots in an old dolls' pram, painted white. Even a pensioned-off pushchair can look quite decorative if it is spray-painted, then filled with flower pots from the seat to the foot-rest.

Plant containers come in many different shapes and sizes

You can grow plants in an old aquarium or in a glass bottle, in the bathroom (provided you choose ones that like little light and a damp atmosphere) and in the kitchen, too. You can take most of them out of doors in the summer, to liven up the look of a terrace, but there are one or two places they simply can't stand: one is being perched on top of a radiator "to keep them warm" and the other is in a really dark corner like the top of the TV set or on the mantelpiece.

You can grow your own house plants from the most unlikely things like carrot tops, avocado stones and orange pips, and you can have fun with a number of old favourites, like geraniums and Michaelmas daisies, by turning them into standard trees. In fact, house plants have a lot to recommend in them for the lazy gardener, because there's scarcely any need to go out of doors, and if you pile them around the window no one will be able to see through to the garden outside, anyway.

Where to place the plants is an important thought – in fact you can grow plants almost anywhere indoors as long as you rotate them every fortnight or so, so that they all get their share of the light. If you use this system, however, don't suddenly switch a plant from relative gloom to the brightness of a window-sill – move it towards the light gradually, for plants can actually suffer from a form of sunburn. How to know if a plant is getting enough light? It will soon tell you by making sad, spindly growth that leans towards the direction from which the light is coming. If your plant is becoming distinctly lop-sided – move it, fast.

There are some house-plants, however, that will grow without any direct sunshine on them at all – decorative ivy (*Hedera*) is one of them, the snake-plant is another. Potted palms don't mind the shade, but are rarely grown now – though they look marvellous in a Victorian-style décor. The creeping fig likes the dark, and so does the periwinkle. Enquire from the shop where you buy the plant – most nurserymen now have a sensible system of labelling house plants with instructions on how to look after them.

All bulb-grown plants such as daffodils, lilies, crocuses and also pot-grown hydrangeas, fuchsias and gardenias need plenty of sun, and when the weather is really warm will benefit enormously from a day spent out of doors.

By the way, if you're growing anything at all exotic on your windowsill, remember that though the central heating may be on, at night in the winter the window itself will be cold. So to save yourself the trouble of nursing a sick plant later on, remember to pull the curtains at night and, if they're at all flimsy, to put a few pages from the day's paper against the window alongside the plants to protect them.

Some house plants are positively hideous – and I include *Sansevieria* (mother-in-law's tongue) as one of these, so take a good look at the finished product before you buy a baby one. I remember being told once in New York that there was a "Very lovely floral tribute" waiting for me in the fridge in my hotel room. It was the ugliest plant I've ever seen – its leaves and its nasty red flowers appeared to be made out of plastic, and to cap it all there was a hideous imitation bee made out of pipe-cleaners nestling among them. It was in fact a strange kind of red lily, and I was very happy to leave it behind for the next guest. Yet on sale, as a small plant, it looks quite attractive.

Geraniums are about the best-tempered, easiest house plants for the lazy gardener to grow, for they positively hate being watered too much, and give a generous show of flowers for your money. Their correct name, as almost everyone must know by now, is zonal pelargonium, and they come in so many different varieties, from those with variegated leaves to the trailing kind, that it is impossible to list them here. If you want a trailing geranium for a hanging basket, though, you must ask for the ivy-leafed kind.

To avoid that terrible straggly look that elderly geraniums affect, take cuttings regularly to get new young plants. It's so easy – you simply take off a growing shoot at joint level, take off the lower leaves, and stick it into sandy soil around the edge of the pot by its "mother". Nip the growing shoots off adult geraniums from time to time, to encourage them to bush outwards rather than grow straight up – that also helps stop straggly growth.

More geraniums die from over-watering than anything else. They need practically no water at all in the winter, and only a moderately moist soil during spring and summer. All geraniums, like other half-hardy plants, benefit enormously from a spell in the garden. Put them out in a flowerbed for a week or so, if you can raise the energy to do so, it will give you stronger-looking plants.

Bulbs like hyacinths, daffodils and narcissus, tulips, too, can very easily be "forced" to bloom early in pots. You need a container with a drainage hole in it and some bulb fibre. Place the bulbs so that they are not touching one another and so that their pointed tops just show above the soil, then put them in a coolish dark place for about a couple of months, to let their roots get on with the job of developing. What you are doing, in fact, is trying to copy the conditions that they would get underground in the garden. A dark, cool cupboard will do, provided you water the pots from time to time, but easier still, you can bury the pots in the garden, where they will get their own moisture. Keen gardeners who are forcing a large number of bulbs often make special plunge beds or boxes of earth, peat or sand.

Once the root system is under way, bring the pots in to a warm, sunny place indoors – they'll think that it is spring and start developing top growth. Hyacinths look better if you leave them growing in a warm but dark place while they are making their flower-spikes. As soon as the plant is put in the sunlight the leaves will change from wilted yellow-white to green, and the plant will romp away.

Experimenting

You can have a lot of fun growing indoor plants in a discarded aquarium or terrarium, provided it has some sort of a top to control ventilation, or in a large glass bottle. The plants thrive on the self-watering principle: as moisture is lost from the leaves and from the soil, it doesn't escape into the atmosphere as it does in a ordinary room, but condenses on the glass and returns

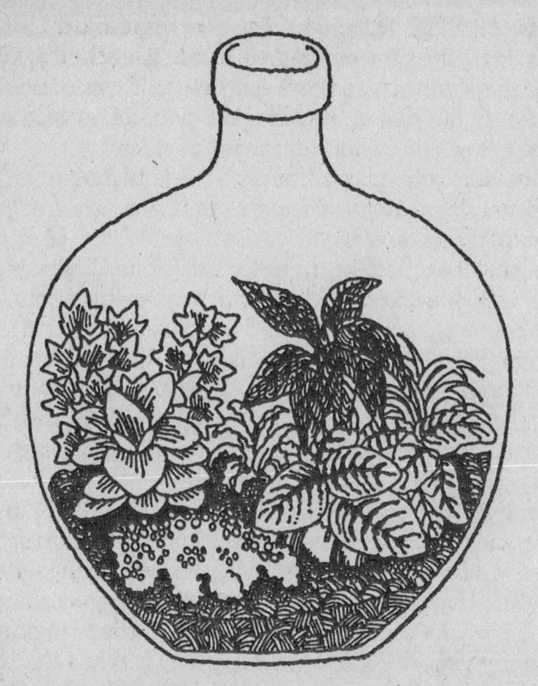

Bottle garden – intriguing to make and a real conversation piece

to make the soil moist again. But remember, you can't keep a bottle garden or terrarium in bright, warm sunlight, or the poor plants will literally cook under the heat.

Any plant that likes a humid atmosphere will take to the bottle – among them ferns, orchids, ivy and some tropical plants. You can also use seedling trees like holly, pine and juniper for a miniature garden effect.

Here's how you fill a bottle: Make a paper funnel through the neck and feed in a layer of charcoal pieces, the kind that you use on a barbecue, or failing that gravel will do. It should form a layer about 2 inches thick. Then top it with 3 inches of brackenish woodland soil, vermiculite, sphagnum moss or peat moss to form a soft bed. Be careful that your materials don't slither down the sides of the bottle and make them messy and muddy. If it's easier, you can use a large spoon lashed to a piece of stick and ladle them in sideways.

Now take the plants that you are planning to use, and wash them, roots and all, so that they are free from old soil. Using a stick or a teaspoon on the end of a piece of wood, "dig" a hole for each one, lower it into place, using tweezers or tongs, then cover the roots with vermiculite or whatever "soil" you have chosen. If you are using anything messy like moss or earth, it's essential that it should not get on the leaves of the plant and spoil them – if this happens, the plant will need brushing clean with a child's paint brush once the earth has dried.

Ideally, the best way to water bottle-garden or terrarium plants is with a fine mist of water. You can buy special appliances for this, but if you have an old perfume atomiser this will do just as well. Using vermiculite as a base, you can even grow a plant in a brandy glass if you give it a lid. It makes an unusual table decoration.

You can produce some plants without any soil or vermiculite at all by simply growing them in water – aquatic plants like miniature water-lilies, for instance, or our old friend the wandering sailor (*Coleus*), which should always be started off in water, anyway. Ivy will grow in water, so will the philodendron. You can grow bulbs like the hyacinth in water, too, provided you either buy from a florist a special-shaped glass to keep the bulb upright, or anchor it in some way in gravel, making sure that the neck of the bulb is out of water. The water needs changing about every 3 weeks, and it's a good idea to put a piece of charcoal in the container to keep it sweet.

You can have a lot of fun growing tropical fruits and other things from pips, seeds and stones. It's not likely that a tree you grow from an orange pip will bear fruit, but it does happen sometimes that miniature oranges appear. Plant several pips together in a pot of sandy soil and keep the pot by a window but in a good temperature – around 65 degrees. Don't make the mistake of burying the pips too deep – that's the main fault that beginners make. They should be no further down in the soil than their own length. Cover the pot with a closed polythene bag while its contents are germinating, so that the soil stays warm and moist, then wait for the shoots to appear. If more than one does come up, choose the strongest-looking and remove the rest. The dwarfing effect of the pot should give you what looks eventually like a miniature citrus tree.

Avocado stones are beasts to get started, but if you can coax them to grow for you, make really handsome houseplants with shiny, waxy leaves. Plant the stone narrow end uppermost in a small pot of sandy soil, or put it in a special vase for growing bulbs and suspend it that way in water so that only the base is wet. Keep it in the light and in a warm place while it puts down roots or, rather, *if* it puts down roots. (I reckon it takes 4 avocado stones to get one plant.)

The most unlikely things like carrot tops and parsnip tops – in fact those from any root vegetable – will grow attractive foliage for you – that of the carrot looks like an ornamental fern. The procedure is perfectly simple and children can easily carry it out; you cut off the tops about 3 inches long, including the leaf stalks, and stand them in a saucer of water until they sprout. Be sure that the water only comes up the sides and not over the top of the piece of carrot. Before long the leaves will fan out and cover the piece of the root.

You can get a very decorative plant by doing the same with the top of a pineapple, but this time it is best to plant it in a pot of moist sand and to cover it with a plastic bag until it has put down roots. Once it has got going it will be happier transferred to a peaty soil to go on growing.

Outdoor variations

Moving out of doors, you can have some very decorative plants around on the patio by simply growing some of the old favourites in standard rather than bush form, so that they make small decorative trees, about the size of a small bay tree. This is done quite easily by training the plant upwards and making sure that it has just one stem instead of several. Fuchsias, Michaelmas daisies, geraniums – in fact, any herbaceous plant with a woody stem – can be made to grow this way.

Start when the plant is quite small, choose the straightest and healthiest specimen you can find, put it in a pot that is slightly larger than the size it needs at the moment, and ram in a bamboo stake that is the height to which you want the plant eventually to grow. Tie the plant to it with raffia, darning wool or something soft and leave it to grow, pinching out any side shoots as they make their appearance. Don't tie the string too tightly – allow room for the stem to swell as the plant grows.

As soon as your now tall, spindly plant has grown almost to the height that you want – with a Michaelmas daisy for instance, 3½ or 4 feet is about right – then pinch off the end of the growing tip and let the first side shoots develop. From now on you encourage it to form a good bushy head, nipping off upward-growing shoots when they begin to look untidy, and making sure that no side shoots are allowed to stay lower down the stem. In time the "trunk" of your flower tree will thicken and the top will become attractive and almost ball-like in shape. Remember that it is important not to remove the leaves in the early stages, but only the shoots along the main stem, especially with fuchsias, which will not thicken well otherwise. All you have to do now is to

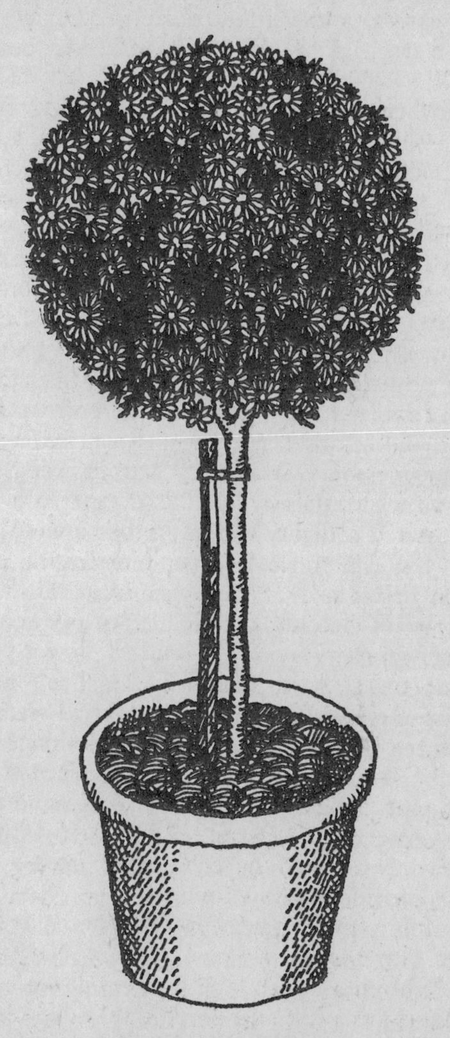

Michaelmas Daisy 'Tree'

shape the plant up and cut it back a little at the beginning of spring, and in due course you'll have a really attractive tree, which you can have inside the house or out.

A strawberry barrel is an attractive and lazy way of growing your own strawberries right outside the back door. Making the barrel up in the first place is rather a chore, but once it has been filled with good soil, it can stay like that for years.

Buy a new barrel, or if it's secondhand make sure it is in a good state, with all the hoops and staves intact ... a barrel that looks as though it might fall apart *will* fall apart when it has the strain of a lot of earth in it. Bore 1-inch holes at uneven intervals all over the barrel, and don't forget to put plenty in the bottom. (You can buy ready-bored wooden barrels at a price, and I have known people make strawberry barrels using a plastic dustbin as the container, but this doesn't look so good.)

Fit a set of 4 ordinary castors on the base of the barrel, so that you can move it around easily, or place the barrel on bricks so that the water can drain away and the soil won't become sour. Then empty some pieces of broken crockery or tiles – crushed flower-pot pieces are ideal – in a layer several inches deep across the bottom of the barrel. Now comes the real secret of success with barrel growing: to get good drainage you need a central "plumbing system", so get a piece of chimney or drain pipe, about 7 inches across, and stand it upright in the centre of the barrel. Now fill it with shingle. (you can buy this by the cubic yard from a builder – he might provide a piece of pipe, too)

Leave the pipe in place for the time being and start to fill the barrel with good quality soil, preferably bought from a local nurseryman, and bulk it out with peat, too. Every time the soil comes level with a hole, poke in a plant and carry on. When the barrel is full, hey presto! take out the pipe (you'll find it easier to do if you have

Once you've set up a strawberry barrel, you can use it for years

been pulling it up as the barrel filled) and you have your drainage system intact.

It doesn't have to be a strawberry barrel, of course; you can have a flower barrel instead, using climbers like clematis and creepers. In fact, you could end up with a positive waterfall of colour all summer, replacing plants as they died down by something new.

OVER TO YOU

I hope this book has persuaded you that gardening need not be all chores, provided you're willing to take an unconventional view of things, and to use your own ideas, too. Come to think of it, you may even get to *like* doing the garden, once it's stocked with the right kind of plants. (I actually went out into my garden voluntarily just now, and did a bit of pottering around.)

As the Americans might say, your garden could become a *fun* place, if only you would let it. There are all sorts of interesting plants around to grow, once you get off the beaten track. I'm experimenting at the moment with some of the weirder herbs that you don't usually see in England, things I need for making curries. Later on I want to try my luck with the Bromeliads, that curious family of plants that grow on trees without being parasitic – orchids and pineapples come into this category. Then there are all those other off-beat things like the Venus flytrap (great fun for the bloodthirsty), the obedient plant, and dittany; North Sea Gas has nothing on this plant, it generates its own – on hot summer days you can actually ignite it without doing it any harm. The effect is rather like the flaming brandy on the Christmas pudding. Then there's the shoo-fly plant, too – but that's another book.

For armchair gardeners who like reading about it, rather than going out and doing it, I must recommend the books of Vita Sackville West (Michael Joseph) who made me realise there was so much more to a garden than hard slog, and whose garden at Sissinghurst, Kent will open your eyes to just what *can* be done with plants.

Making Things Grow, by Thalassa Cruso (Michael Joseph) is another delightful armchair book on indoor gardening, while if you're interested to hear that the dreaded ground elder is actually good as a medicine for your kidneys, take a look at *How to Enjoy Your Weeds* by Audrey Lynne Hatfield (Muller). And if you want to start at square one, and learn what gardening is all about, get hold of a copy of A. G. Hellyer's *The Amateur Gardener*–it's out of print at the moment, but you should be able to get it at your local public library.

INDEX